A YEAR IN THE GARDEN

A YEAR IN THE GARDEN

Four Seasons of Texture, Color, and Beauty

Text by Theodore James, Jr.
Photographs by Harry Haralambou

Viking Studio

ACKNOWLEDGMENTS

We are very grateful to the following people for their kind assistance and support: Alice Levien, Joanne Woodle, Coni Cross, Roberta Lee, John Greene, Iris Megadubia, Jay Applegate, Angelica Lejuge, Rosa Petals, Barbara Moorehouse, Katerina Haralambou, Andrulla Zinon, Yiota Pappas, Chloe and Olivia Pappas-Kelly, Helen Jacobs, Stanley Plum, Paul Jacobs, Stella Biniaris, Cathy Zgaljic, George Philippou, and Rolanda PortoVerde. We would like to thank particularly Ken Ruzicka for the magnificent home he created for our frogs, for Koi, and for filet of sole. We would also like to thank The Netherland's Flower Bulb Information center. Finally, we are most grateful to Cyril Nelson, Adrian Zackheim, Chris Sweet, Pat Adams, and Elissa Altman and to our dear friend and agent, Roz Cole.

VIKING STUDIO
Published by the Penguin Group
Penguin Putnam Inc., 375 Hudson Street, New York, New York 10014, U.S.A.
Penguin Books Ltd, 80 Strand, London WC2R 0RL, England
Penguin Books Australia Ltd, 250 Camberwell Road, Camberwell, Victoria 3124, Australia
Penguin Books Canada Ltd, 10 Alcorn Avenue, Toronto, Ontario, Canada M4V 3B2
Penguin Books India (P) Ltd, 11 Community Centre, Panchsheel Park, New Delhi—110 017, India
Penguin Books (N.Z.) Ltd, Cnr Rosedale and Airborne Roads, Albany, Auckland, New Zealand
Penguin Books (South Africa) (Pty) Ltd, 24 Sturdee Avenue, Rosebank, Johannesburg 2196, South Africa

Penguin Books Ltd, Registered Offices:
Harmondsworth, Middlesex, England

First published in 2003 by Viking Studio,
a member of Penguin Putnam Inc.

1 3 5 7 9 10 8 6 4 2

Copyright © Theodore James, Jr., 2003
Photographs copyright © Harry Haralambou, 2003
All rights reserved

ISBN 0-670-89669-1

CIP available

This book is printed on acid-free paper. ∞
Printed in China
Set in Adobe Garamond
Designed by Jaye Zimet

For our dear friend Sue Blair

My life as a gardener began during childhood, when I was first exposed to horticultural wonders by my late grandmother. She had a lovely garden, and I spent many hours there helping her weed, picking flowers, deadheading, and getting my feet wet in the world of plants. That included accompanying her on her forays into gardens of perfect strangers and aiding in her bald-faced acquisition of rose cuttings that she simply took, without permission, from any garden she spotted that had a rose bush in it she wanted. Sometimes I was the hit man on those excursions. I was only four or five, an "enchanting" child, according to my only surviving uncle, and everybody seemed to be very happy that I had taken a rose for a cutting. Not to worry, inevitably her victims became her friends. And I did learn at that point that gardeners are generous and love to share not only plants but also advice and information with others. That was just before World War II.

Then came the war and Victory Gardens. In suburban Chatham, New Jersey, everybody had a Victory Garden. Backyards, empty lots, windowsills were filled with rows and containers of string beans, tomatoes, lettuce, beets, carrots, early peas, melons, cucumbers, and two vegetables that were new to me, kohlrabi and Swiss chard. Many of us children had small gardens of our own, proudly pulling the first radish from the ground in late spring. And we also helped with the work. After all, it was for the war effort and, as the saying went, "Him who don't work, don't eat."

Introduction

Further, in our fourth-grade class, we had a "clean plate club," so as not to waste food, much of which was rationed. Quite expectedly, I was the president, because at that stage of my life I had the relentless desire to run everything. Every day, each one of us had to report whether or not we had cleaned our plates. Stars were put on charts in gold, silver, and red. Gold meant that you had cleaned your plate. Silver meant that you didn't eat your spinach, which was somewhat acceptable. Red meant that you didn't eat much of anything and wasted food. It was all on the honor system, and we children took it very seriously and seemed to be quite honest about our daily performance. Our teacher was a fine French Canadian lady named Esther Daigle, who remained a friend of my late mother's and mine until she died in the 1970s. After the flag salute and the prayer, she would tell us all not to forget the "starving French war orphans." For whatever reason, we didn't.

The women of Chatham canned and preserved from their gardens to fill their larders. This was done in pressure cookers at that time. One of our neighbors had made one out of heavy-duty metal, which had about twenty screws on the top that had to be secured with a wrench. My father named it "the Iron Lung." All of the neighbors would borrow it for a

Opposite page: The soil on the North Fork is the best this side of Kansas. Everything grows out here. Here, groves of dwarf flowering trees color the landscape in spring.

few days to can string beans, relishes, tomatoes, and so forth. Often the women would work together on canning, many times quite late into the night. All of this was to help the war effort and to defeat Nazi Germany and Hitler, his sidekick Benito Mussolini, and Tojo from the Land of the Rising Sun. I do remember, back in 1944 or so, when a hurricane was headed in our direction, armies of women, including my mother and grandmother, out in the community Victory Garden (everybody had their own allocated space) gathering produce, as I recall, primarily cabbage. To this day I do not understand why they were more concerned about their cabbage than anything else. After the war, most people continued with their Victory Gardens since they had become accustomed to the fresh quality of the food.

My years at college produced only one vague stab at gardening. I did go and buy two philodendrons for my room, which I shared with two other fellows. I told them I had bought them, now it was their job to water them. Alas, they were dead in one month, and I was so enraged at my roommates, I called them both spoiled rich kids who had been picked up after all of their lives, and then threw and smashed the pots in the fireplace. They remain close friends and, according to their wives, still do not pick up after themselves.

By 1973, I was living in New York and had spent fifteen years of my life carving out my career as a writer-journalist. I spent that year abroad working on a project about the grand hotels of Europe. It was a glorious summer and a glorious assignment since I was living in and collecting recipes and memorabilia from more than thirty hotels on the Continent and beyond. Then came 1974. That was the turning point. I had no plans to leave the city at all that summer. That did not sit well with me because Manhattan during summer is hot, humid, smelly, and uninhabitable, although on occasional summer weekends it can be quite delightful. And by that time, I had more than a hundred houseplants in the place, on windowsills, under lights—my own indoor mini-garden. I was about to turn forty and, looking at my houseplant collection, realized that I needed a piece of land on which to create a garden on a civilized scale. I did have a little cash stashed away and knew that I would probably fritter it away on new stereo equipment, a trip abroad, and too much pricey food and drink. It was then that I remembered a saying about ambitious young Englishmen. "They come from the country and go to the city to seek their fortune so that they can afford to move back to the country." By no means was there a fortune involved but there was enough to take this quite adventurous step. It was then that I started to look for a piece of country property to buy, one where I could escape the city and also garden.

I found it in Peconic, on the North Fork of Long Island, which at that time was indeed a backwash, an anachronism, totally out of synch with the present, and undiscovered by the

A typical scene of the water-laced North Fork. When people ask where it is, we always say, "East of Eden." *Rosa rugosa* has naturalized here at Goldsmith's Inlet.

What could be more beautiful than looking out over our wetlands at a group of swans gliding by in the moonlight? North Forkers often go to the beaches to view the beauty of the full moon.

hordes in Manhattan. It was rural, beautiful, and I immediately felt comfortable here. I later learned that when local people said they went to "town" for the weekend, they meant Boston, not New York. The North Fork had truly been an isolated area for the better part of its history. Ethnically, there were the descendants of the original English immigrants, who arrived in 1648. And there were Irish, Portuguese, and Polish immigrants who followed.

One Monday, a real estate agent, to whom I will be forever grateful for seeing to it that I did indeed get the house, called me and said, "I have just what you are looking for. The house is eighteenth century; it is on one acre of land on a country road, and the price is right." I told her I would come out the following day. She said, "You must come today. It will be gone by tomorrow." She held off other potential buyers until I got there, and she was right, it was a perfect house for me—a small half-Cape, built close to the road, with a one-acre piece of land behind it. And, there were a number of rather grand trees on the property, including a 150-year-old yew. At any rate I gave her the down payment, and then on July 24th, I took title to the house that was to become my life for the last twenty-five years.

There was nothing here but the house, uninsulated, with windows that needed replacement, walls that needed replacement, floors that needed replacement, underpinnings that

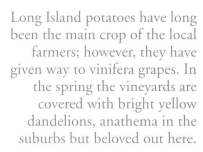

Long Island potatoes have long been the main crop of the local farmers; however, they have given way to vinifera grapes. In the spring the vineyards are covered with bright yellow dandelions, anathema in the suburbs but beloved out here.

needed replacement, and a great many small trees and weeds that had to be cleared in order for me to start my garden. And the house was covered with about one inch of stucco, painted a pea green, which some misguided owner had put on back in the 1920s. But, there was the wonderful yew tree. I decided at that point to name my house "Yew II," which has stuck for the past twenty-five years. Plus, there was the best soil this side of Kansas. Everything grows here. If you spit out a peach pit, not only do you have a peach tree the next year but you also have peaches on it. And it is in Zone 7A, which means that I don't have to dig gladiolas. My camellias grow outdoors all winter and bloom magnificently; fig trees do not have to be wrapped and insulated or buried; crape myrtle is vigorous here; and my *Magnolia grandiflora*, which I call Scarlet's Revenge, offers its enormous blooms sporadically through the summer.

My late parents both wanted to come out to look it over, so along with my basset hound, William, they came out. When mother walked in the house, she burst into tears. My grandmother had done the same thing when she walked into my first and only apartment in the West Village back in 1959. However, my father thought that it was a sound investment. I pointed out to my mother that the paneling, mantle, and other woodwork, which were covered with ten layers of paint, could be restored to their original Maine pine, mellow honey color. And the wide-beamed floors were waiting only to be sanded and refinished. The glass in the windows was all handblown, and quite delicate. Eventually this had to be replaced. Under the layers of ceiling, I knew there were hand-hewn beams waiting to be uncovered. There was a Dutch oven adjoining one of the fireplaces. The possibilities were quite wonderful, I thought. Today the front of the house is graced with a bronze landmark plaque. It is very gratifying because it was not a checkbook restoration. Blood, sweat, tears, and armies of friends helped through the years. It is said that both Thomas Jefferson and James Madison visited the house after the American Revolution when they were on their way to Boston. Apparently, the cash crop on the East End in those days was wheat. A nasty disease had attacked the wheat and devastated the crops. Thomas Jefferson had developed a disease-resistant variety of wheat and brought seeds with him to give to the East End farmers. He and Madison stayed at a house that is less than a mile from here.

Eventually, my doubting mother did agree that it was a very special house and a very special part of the world. My parents grew to love the North Fork, to the point that they sold their house in New Jersey, bought the property next door, and built their own house. When they did that, many said to me, "It must be terrible having your parents live right next door to you." I said, "No, it isn't at all. There is a Laundromat over there, a take-out restaurant, and an after-hours bar. That's not so bad."

Even in the dead of winter there is beauty in the landscape. Here, amid the mud and ice of February, is what is left of a crop of Brussels sprouts.

A few days after the closing, one of my neighbors came over to introduce himself. He grew potatoes down the street and told me that about five years before, two sisters, both maiden ladies, lived out their lives in the house. Their name was Wells, and the house had been in that family for more than two hundred years. My neighbor told me that one day he saw Miss Millie, the younger of the two, out in the yard digging with a shovel. He came over and asked what she was doing. She told him that her sister had died over the hot-air grate inside and she was digging a grave for her. He said, "You can't bury her here. She has to be embalmed and prepared for burial in a graveyard." Miss Millie replied, "Well that's how we've always done it here." The next day I was out in the back digging a hole for a dogwood tree that I had bought. And, lo and behold, there was a very large bone in the ground. I am sure it was that of a cow or a horse, but nonetheless it was somewhat unsettling. Years later, my neighbor did confess that it was a prank.

Hundreds of artifacts have surfaced here through the years. Many broken pieces of old china, all manner of bottles, silver spoons, coins, doll arms, keys, and so forth. The prize, however, has been a shiny brass medallion, dated 1763. On one side, there is an engraved coat of arms with a crown above it. The words, "In Memory of the Good Old Days" are inscribed around the edge. On the other side, there is an image of King George II of England with the words in Latin, *Georgius II dei gratia.* The Treaty of Paris, in which France ceded Canada and other parts of its empire to Great Britain, was signed in 1763. During the American Revolution, the North Fork was strongly Tory and very sympathetic to the Crown.

Buying the house in Peconic was the best investment of time, money, and imagination that I have ever made. After only one year of enduring a split personality, that of a city rat and a country mouse, I took the key money for my rent-controlled apartment and moved out here full time. And I have never regretted it. In those days, I was writing books and articles, primarily about New York. I had had a number of books published that focused on the city. *Fifth Avenue* was one, *The Empire State Building* another. But in Peconic, there was no Fifth Avenue. The tallest structure here was an old whaling captain's house, which had a widow's walk up top, and no glitter circuit or beautiful people to write about. But there was one acre of fabulous soil surrounding the house. And so began my career as a garden writer. Within a year or so I met my photographer colleague and friend Harry Haralambou, and we teamed up to write books and plan the gardens here. Once those decisions had been made, my life seemed to fall into place.

We hope that you will enjoy the story of a year in the life of our garden. We have tried to share the joys, the pitfalls, the advice, and the gratification that we have experienced with you. This book is not intended to be a definitive book on gardening, but rather a very personal view of our own experience, written in the hopes that it may bring joy to you in your own pursuit of gardening. For us, gardening is our work that we love to do and not our toil. Our garden is paradise. Welcome!

The sunsets over the North Fork, in this case over Richmond Creek, just a short walk from the house, are legendary. Screaming pinks, oranges, yellows, and purples give them a somewhat lurid look.

There are several ways to approach the planning of a garden. One can sit down with a large piece of graph paper and create a scheme. At most, this design effort might take several months, off and on. Once that is done, planting and installing landscape features proceed. Others with less time, or experience, hire landscape designers to plan the scheme and install it. Our garden evolved. We didn't really have a detailed master plan, but we did have some basic concepts in mind when we started. We knew many kinds of plants that we wanted in our garden, as well as landscape features. For the most part, through the years, additions and changes were made as we saw fit.

Our garden is always in transition, in much the same way that a human life is. Like us, plants are born, they thrive, they reproduce, they get older and need rejuvenation, and they die. Each stage of the garden and of individual plants has its own special beauty. And here, there is always one area that, for one reason or other, is undergoing drastic change. There are many reasons why this is true. Sometimes we are not happy with combinations, or with certain plants. Sometimes the plants outgrow the garden. Sometimes they die. Every year, we make changes with details that we are not happy with or that simply do not work for us. Like our garden, because of the constant change, no garden is ever perfect and no garden is ever finished.

One of our basic concepts is what we call the mini-estate premise. That is, the garden is a scaled-down version of the classic great estate gardens, with many small "rooms" that are interconnected, leading from one to another. These spaces are all defined, with paths, entrances, and borders. Since the property here is just shy of an acre, and since we did want so many different kinds of gardens, this was the route we took. So, we have an alpine garden, a water garden, a shade garden, a perennial garden, a Nisei or Japanese-American garden, a shrub garden, and a woodland garden. We even have a number of secret places, where guests who seek privacy for whatever reason can go off by themselves and be alone.

We have mixed formal and informal gardens, areas with long vistas, and those that are very contained. In order to accommodate all of these plantings, we have concentrated on finding and planting dwarf shrubs and small trees, along with dwarf versions of many of the taller perennials. When people first walk through the garden, they are always surprised to learn that it is less than one acre. All say, "It seems much, much larger than that."

The second concept we like is that a garden should be a series of events, spectacles, and occurrences that continue throughout the four seasons. These events are created by the gardener: dazzling displays, garden design, selection of cultivars. Or they are influenced by

Opposite: The series of photographs that follows shows how one of our gardens has evolved through the years. The first photograph shows the initial patio installation during the first year of the project.

The following year, we added a Romanesque brick arch, and started a crack garden amid the patio stones. Notice that by the fourth year, the euonymus hedge, which was installed to contain the garden, has begun to serve its purpose. The fourth photo shows the garden at maturity, at about five years old. And the last, taken ten years later, reveals the beauty of the same garden during the winter, covered with snow.

Here is another example of how our garden has evolved. The first photograph shows the initial idea. We wanted a grass pathway leading into the perennial garden. We extended the euonymus hedge on the right and added some boxwood on the left. The following year, we found an old gate, appropriate for the vintage of the house, at a yard sale and installed that. However, the pathway looked lopsided. Two years later, we yanked out the euonymus and planted box in its place, so that both sides of the path were lined with it. With the addition of the brick pedestals and the urns, the grass pathway now has a finished look and is quite elegant.

events which happen in nature: the changing of the seasons, wildlife in the garden, birth and death, health and disease, and weather factors, such as drought, hurricanes, heavy downpours, strong winds, and extreme cold.

In that sense it is up to us, the gardeners, to plan and execute these events to our own liking and thus become a part of the yearly life cycle of the garden. Of course, a gardener cannot control the events of nature but can aid, enhance, and abet many of them. I always remember a comment made by Penelope Hobhouse, the British gardener and author. Someone asked her if she took credit for a chance combination of plants that just happened in the garden. She replied, "Yes I do." They asked her why and she said, "Because I had the sense to leave it alone."

Most gardens reflect their owners, and we wanted ours to act as a setting for our style of living, which on rare occasions has its formal side but almost always is informal. It is very much like a theater, with the play all about the joys, triumphs, disappointments, and sorrows of life. Birth, death, illness, weather, celebrations, and friendship are all different scenes in the play. The play is in four acts: spring, summer, fall, and winter, with many scenes in each act. The sets change with each act, as does the music, the lighting, and the characters.

We call it a theater of life. The score of the play is the sound of the wind, the rain, the birds, running water, the laughter, and the tears. The lighting is the sun, the heavens, the

This garden, designed by our friend Connie Cross, is interesting during spring, summer, fall, and winter. The gazebo is the focus. The plantings change during the course of the seasons.

Here you see how our rock garden evolved into a combination of rock garden and water garden. The first photograph shows what the rock garden looked like before the water garden was installed. The second shows the waterfall added to the rock garden. The last two show the water garden during late summer and winter.

In this series, a section of the fence is planned so that it is interesting in all of the seasons. In the spring, *Clematis montana rubens* offers lovely pink blossoms, followed by deep green foliage in summer. In the fall, *Cotoneaster horizontalis* berries decorate the fence, and in the winter, the snow-laden branches of *Parthecunossis* (Boston ivy) offer lattice-patterned jigsaw.

moon, the clouds, or the lighting you choose to install. The lead actor, the "star" shall we say, is you, the gardener, and those with whom you have designed this setting for life. Other characters come and go throughout the play, the visitors, sometimes in great numbers as during garden tours, sometimes for celebrations and parties, sometimes alone, but they are always coming and going. While on our stage, the cast of characters is enhanced and interacts with the set, or stage of life, as actors in the theater do. They behave differently than usual when they are wandering through the garden. They are contemplative, they absorb the surrounding beauty, and they seem to take on new dimensions. They are happy.

There are many minor characters: birds, butterflies, lightning bugs, water spiders, dragonflies, rabbits, quail, fox, possums, squirrels, and yes, voles and moles, all making their appearances during the course of the play. And there are props: archways, gazebos, container plantings, garden furniture, urns, patios, stone constructions, and waterfalls, manmade additions to nature's scheme.

We have also provided a dramatic entrance to our theater. When you walk in through the gate, you are confronted with a long vista, stretching from the very front of the property to the rear. A charming statue of a cherub, or *putti,* sits at the far end of the vista. Behind the statue is a mirror that gives the illusion that the garden goes on and on. Above it is an

Notice how the mirror adds a lush reflection of the garden as a backdrop for the window box plantings. One of the nice things about window boxes is that you can change the plantings every year. The mirrors are also whimsical, because they startle visitors when they see their own reflections as they walk by.

Looking toward the rear of the property, the archway leads the eye to the charming statue of the cherub. The first photo in the series reveals the spectacular May blooming of the *Laburnum* x *watereri* 'Vossii' trained to an arbor in the background. The second includes the lush foliage of late spring when hollyhocks are in bloom. The third shows white angel's trumpets in bloom, along with the lush foliage of summer, and the last is the vista after a winter snow. Notice how the purple archway contrasts so nicely with the snow. Using color in structures gives a winter garden visual interest.

arbor that is covered with the stunning yellow panicles of laburnum in the spring. This makes the garden appear as though it is considerably larger than it really is. As visitors walk from front to back, they are on our stage for all to see. Even those least likely to succumb to gesture, exaggerate their entrances, as though they were part of a theatrical event.

Our garden theater presents a microcosm of life. We have had many blessed events in the garden: the birth of rabbits in the rock garden; birds, of course, all over the place; fish and frogs in the water garden; and garter snakes in the barn. Two Carolina wrens built their nest in a flower pot in the barn, and the young birds gathered at the window daily, waiting for their mother to come with food.

We have regular visitors. In the fall, flocks of geese and ducks fly over the garden, coming and going to their roosting places, and they are always on time. Major spectacles occur, such as the evening millions of monarch butterflies settled on a large maple tree, which had already turned brilliant yellow. The entire tree was a fluttering mass of rust and yellow. One day we came home and found an adorable little fawn in our rock garden, with his mother not far away. We now have a stockade fence surrounding the property so we never have visits from deer, indeed a blessing since they'll eat everything in sight if they are hungry. A flock of about two hundred pine siskins spent New Year's Day at our feeders one winter. Brilliant yellow and black evening grosbeaks have visited, and one year we had both an indigo bunting and a blue grosbeak at one of the feeders all during the day. Birdhouses are filled with sparrows, who stay all year long and have brood after brood. I did learn that sparrows tend to stay in one place, and when they do, they develop a birdcall that is particular only to that area. One day I discovered that I could hand-feed chickadees and mourning doves. You can imagine the magic when the first chickadee landed on my outstretched palm, took a seed, and flew away. He was as light as a feather, and I could barely feel his weight. My late father used to like to sit in the rose garden and take a snooze. He always wore a wide-brimmed straw hat to keep the sun from his face. While he was asleep we could place a handful of sunflower seeds on the brim of his hat, and then watch the chickadees fly onto it, eating their feast while perched on the brim. He was never aware that they were doing so.

There is also death in the garden, destruction by storms, disease, and old age. Right now, we are trying to cope with a sick shrub, a Sargent's weeping hemlock, spraying it with dormant oil in the spring and hoping for the best. The hemlock suffers from a new disease called wooly adelgid that has only surfaced in the past ten years. It is a magnificent shrub that was planted more than twenty years ago, and if it dies, it will almost be like losing a pet or a friend. Fortunately, it does appear as though we are winning the battle and that it might well survive. But we have developed a philosophy about the life and death of the plants that has helped us to deal with the realities of our own life and death, as well as the loss of pets, friends, and family. Plants are born, they grow, they reproduce, and they die, just as human beings do.

When one surrounds oneself with the beauty of a garden, we human beings take our proper place in the natural scheme of things. We become a part of nature and eventually realize that we are just one small part of God's world, no more important and no less important than any other living thing. It is a humbling experience to abandon human arrogance in favor of the larger scheme of what life is all about.

Perhaps the most prevalent criticism of American gardens and gardeners by those abroad is that we lack a spirit of adventure. Whether it is because we are insecure with our judgments or lack imagination, I don't know. But turn over a new leaf right away. Don't be afraid to try something new and different. For instance, in decorating a living room, a combination of purple and orange is likely to be jarring. However in the garden, the same combination, perhaps because we are dealing with color that is alive rather than dead, can be very striking. In fact, it is a favorite combination among sophisticated gardeners. Since our garden does evolve, we are always trying something new and experiment frequently.

Here is an example of a successful experiment. Early in the spring, about twenty years ago, a friend of mine who hybridized rhododendrons and was quite well known throughout the rhododendron world passed away. His widow was selling his experimental rhododendrons. None were named nor was there any manner of identification of color on any of them. I have since learned that it is a very bad idea to buy, accept, or plant any cultivar that is not identified. You have absolutely no idea what it looks like, how tall it will grow, whether or not it is invasive, or whether it will suit the space and location you select for it. Despite warnings, I did buy about a dozen rhododendrons and deciduous azaleas and installed a small rhododendron garden. After two or three years, they began to bloom. They were all in purples, mauves, shocking pinks, oranges, salmon, and rust, and they were getting bigger and bigger. I thought they looked awful, but was hesitant to yank them out because of the personal connection.

A European friend came to visit the garden one day and stopped at the rhododendron section, which was in full bloom. She is an art historian, quite avant-garde in her tastes, who tends to be very enthusiastic when she comes upon an unusual combination of colors, be it in a work of art, on a dinner plate, in a boudoir, on clothes and jewelry, or in a garden. She stood there with her mouth ajar and said, "It's magnificent!" I said, "It isn't at all. It is ghastly!" She said, "No! No! It's pure Gauguin!" I realized that she was indeed correct, the

These companion photographs of a pathway in our garden were taken in spring and early fall. Notice how we have installed plantings that are lovely to look at during both seasons.

If you are aware of small, unexpected events in your garden, and keep a sharp eye out for lovely visual experiences, you will find spider webs covered with droplets of morning dew.

colors were those that Gauguin had used in his work, and so from that day on I have always proudly referred to that particular garden as the Gauguin garden. And I have grown to love it. In fact, I even try to enhance the color combination with other plants from time to time.

Sometimes things don't go as planned, however. Often a friend or relative gives you a plant that you may not think is quite right for the garden, but it does have personal meaning to you. By all means, put it somewhere. My grandmother loved lilies of the valley. Before she died, she gave a lot of them to my mother, who planted them in New Jersey, and then brought some out here to our garden. I didn't really have a place for them, so I put them in a temporary location that has turned out to be just the right place, and they are there to this day. Several years ago, I was going to New Jersey, and I dug some up and planted them on my grandmother's grave.

Another time, after traveling to Scotland and Ireland and seeing the fabulous sky-blue poppies, *Meconopsis betonicifolia,* in bloom, I thought I would try to grow them. In that part of the world, as well as in our Pacific Northwest, where the cool, moist summers are appropriate for their culture, they thrive. I was determined to bring them to bloom, despite the fact that absolutely everyone and everything I read said that they would not grow nor would they bloom in our Long Island climate of hot, humid, and dry summers. The first year I tried ordering some plants and installing them in the garden. I did that, and inside of three weeks they were all dead. The following year, I tried growing them from seed. They did germinate, and I did plant them, however again they failed. The third year, I ordered some larger plants and installed them in a sunny location, close to the house, where I could give them the intensive care they needed. Much to my amazement, and quite against all odds and warnings, they did bloom. And beautifully. They did not, however, make it through the following winter.

Once you have planted your garden, we strongly advise you to get involved in some of the maintenance. Don't be afraid to weed, dig, mow the lawn, or water. Of course, you may not want to do that all the time, but once in a while it is a good idea because you will see things in the garden and on the plants that you would not otherwise see. When you get close to the garden, you will see lovely spider webs with sparkling droplets of water on them, and all manner of insects. You will see patterns of nature that you don't normally see. Perhaps your dogwoods have seeded themselves under the tree. That means you can transplant them and in several years have a full-fledged dogwood to plant somewhere on your property. Be sure to take walks at all different times of the day. The garden is quite beautiful at dawn in the mist, or at sunset bathed in color, or during rainstorms or snowstorms. And remember that if you have a garden there is always something to look forward to. For example, if you plant bulbs or new shrubs or perennials in the fall, in the spring you will enjoy the beauty of the plantings. How gratifying that is. In spring you look forward to the garden in summer, then to the fall garden, and finally to winter. In many ways, particularly as you get older, the garden keeps you going.

Here are a few things to keep in mind as you plan your garden. Gardening can be addictive. However, it is perhaps the only addiction that is truly healthy. Listen to visitors when they come to see the garden. Very often, because you are so close to it all, you lose objectivity and miss things that others will notice. Don't be afraid to borrow ideas from other people's gardens, from books and articles, and from photographs. All gardeners do it, and you don't have to explain where or why you did. Although hardly desirable, having had Lyme disease is a status symbol in the gardening world. And what gardener, no matter how grand, has ever been ashamed of having occasional dirt under the fingernails? Finally, keep in mind that you are never closer to God than when you are down on your hands and knees working in the garden.

Dawn in any garden, with the mysterious morning mists enveloping the details, is not to be missed. Be sure to get up early every now and then to experience its beauty.

Long ago Chaucer concluded that April was the cruelest month. It tempts the spirit with glorious spring-like days, and then slams the soul with snow, ice, rain, and leaden skies. The landscape in early spring is bleak. The trees stand gaunt and stark, weeks away from leafing out. But week by week, the progression of spring, which begins with a trickle of spring color, turns into a flood of plants displaying their glorious bloom.

Spring comes to the North Fork in many ways other than by the calendar. Wild asparagus pokes through the snow at the banks of local creeks. Farmers here call it "sparrow grass," which derives from the Elizabethan pronunciation of the word. It has survived since the first immigrants brought it with them from England when they settled here in 1640. Flounder swim into and up the creeks. They only stay for about two weeks before returning to deep salt water, but during that period they are there for the taking. The swans in the local creeks are busy defining their territory since they will soon mate and produce a healthy crop of cygnets. The honking Canada geese, which increase in number every year, once again fly in formation from their nesting areas to feeding areas. They go one way in the morning and return in the evening, always at sunset, and always making a racket. Snow fences are dismantled and stored away for the next year. At the nurseries, row upon row of trees are bagged and burlapped, ready for shipping. At the vineyards, the

Spring in the Garden

grapes are pruned by hand; and on farms, plows run up and down rows, leaving trails of last year's leftover potatoes behind as they prepare the soil for this year's crop. Spinach and leeks, the first crops of the year, are already at the farm stands, and peas will follow soon.

It is the busiest time of year for all gardeners and the beginning of a year in the life of a garden. There are many chores to do. You must clean up the garden, install new plantings, order seeds and annuals, and move other plants. It seems endless. In a way, you do become a slave to the garden. That all abates as the season goes on, and for all gardeners it is an exciting time. But the more you get done in the fall, the more you have time to enjoy the spring garden.

Some tasks are essential, and you should tend to them every spring. Through the winter, the ground freezes and thaws, and very often, small potholes appear in the lawn or walking areas. I call them "mouse graves," and I learned how to deal with them the hard way, by twisting my ankle in them. I prefer to think that evil creatures of the night, probably trolls, come and dig small graves all over the garden to bury mice. However, they never find the mice and thus leave the graves open. Two years ago in early spring, I fell and

Opposite: A typical springtime scene on the North Fork. Locally grown nursery stock is dug and bagged and burlapped and waits to be shipped to eager gardeners all over the Northeast. The luminous light on the East End gives this photograph a very special visual quality.

twisted my ankle three times. For weeks I had to hobble around. So, be sure to fill in all of those mouse graves to avoid painful accidents.

On mild days, take the time to walk around the garden. It is easy to see the basic structure of your landscape at this time of year. Make decisions about what and when to move and where to move it. Take a notebook with you and note any changes in design you think might be a good thing. Think about making a list of plants that will enhance the late-winter and early-spring garden: dwarf conifers, berry-bearing plants, and plants with special bark interest. Spring is also the major planting season, the time to shop for and to plant new shrubs, perennials, summer bulbs, and annuals.

It is also time to start tuberous begonias, caladiums, and *Colocasia* (elephant's ear) indoors. We do this every year since all three plants are essential to dressing up shady areas during the summer months. The vibrant colors of begonias and the brilliantly variegated foliage of caladiums are a godsend to all who have shady areas in their gardens, and *Colocasia* add a flamboyantly tropical touch to any garden. To start begonias, just fill a large deep tray with peat moss, moisten it so that it is damp throughout, set the tubers in the medium with the rounded side up, place in a brightly lit spot out of direct sun, and wait and watch. After about two weeks little sprouts will appear on the surface of the tubers. At this point, begin to water very moderately and continue to do so. After all danger of frost is past, when the begonias should be about 8 inches high, they are ready to set out into the garden. You start caladiums and *Colocasia* in pots at the same time, and by the time all danger of frost is past, they are about 8 inches high and ready to set out into the garden. Little maintenance is required during the growing season. A little fertilizer, reasonable moisture, and a shady location are all your plants need to thrive. And what wonderful rewards! Shady places that are not very friendly to flowering plants dazzle with the bright colors of the begonias and the flamboyant foliage of the caladiums.

Begonia tubers are grown in Belgium, not Holland. Each year there is an extravagant display of them in the Grand-Place in Brussels. In Ghent, every several years, during the Belgian Floriade (a flower festival), begonias are used as roses are at the Rose Bowl parade and celebration: for carpets of flowers, on floats, and fashioned into all manner of figures and architectural landmarks.

Spring is also the time of year when many open their gardens for charity tours. May and June are the usual months because almost all gardens are at their very best during this period. We have done this four times. But be advised, if you are considering doing it, that it is always a great deal of work, often taking weeks. The entire garden must be edged, mulched, and everything put in order so that it looks its best. After all, it is your garden and you want to dazzle the guests. It is a big job, but ultimately, having several hundred enthusiasts, many of them quite knowledgeable, enjoying your creation is very gratifying. It is like having a very large garden party, without having to worry about serving food and drink. If you are a gardener, it is a good idea to take in some of these tours. You will learn about what grows in your particular area, get ideas about plantings in your own garden, and meet people who are also interested in gardening.

I remember one incident during a garden tour here with special fondness. A very pretty, but shy, young woman came to me as she was leaving the garden and said, "Oh Mr. James, I hope you don't mind, but I sat on the bench for over half an hour just looking at your water garden and making believe it was all mine." Another lady could not resist pulling out weeds. I went over to her and she said, "Oh please forgive me, but I am a gardener, and I can't resist pulling out the weeds." I said, "Madame, you are welcome in my garden anytime."

Another time, the Hampton Alliance, a large garden club from the Hamptons over on the South Fork, came to visit the gardens of the North Fork. There were more than five hundred of them on the tour. One of the guests got all excited about the garden. He was bellowing, "This is a wonderful garden! They've got six kinds of boxwood!" But perhaps the most memorable incident was the visit of a lady who was a grande dame in every sense of the word. She arrived with her white-gloved entourage of five "ladies-in-waiting," who were somewhat cowed by her presence, dutifully trailing behind her. She too wore white gloves and a straw garden hat covered with daffodils, and she carried a cane. Word buzzed around the garden that she had arrived. We were terrified. What would she think? Would she like the garden?

I thought it best to introduce myself, so I went over to welcome her. We shook hands, and she turned and banged her cane on a flagstone saying, "Now this is a garden! I see some weeds over there." This was followed by, "Mr. James, I want you to call me first thing in the morning. We have things to talk about." Needless to say, I was relieved. She liked the garden very much. We were up to snuff and had made it in the big time! The lady knew from a lifetime of experience that gardens must have flaws. Perfectly manicured gardens are cold and impersonal. But flaws, as with people, make the garden warm and human.

Spring is also the time to clean out existing birdhouses and to add more. Every year all of ours are occupied. Chickadees, sparrows, and titmice nest in them. The sweet little gray-peaked, tufted titmice, we learned, have a nesting arrangement that is quite different from other songbirds. They nest in threes. We hesitate to even think what is going on in that birdhouse every spring. Every year we cut up string and odd pieces of yarn and hang it on a

By midspring, goldfinches shed their khakis and don their brilliant yellow and black plumage. Here they snack at a thistle feeder that we have placed on a flowering apricot tree. ■ A late snowfall does no harm to the species tulips and the mini-daffodils. They are hardy and will not be damaged or frostbitten.

tree. The birds use it to make their nests. Of course, the robins arrive from down south, where they have been sunning themselves all winter. However, recently, we have seen more and more of them staying here in winter, perhaps a sign of global warming. Mockingbirds also remain through the winter.

In spring, male goldfinches shed their drab khaki plumage and get all dressed up in splendid brilliant yellow and black. They enjoy thistle, so we have several thistle feeders hanging here and there. As the flowering trees go in and out of bloom, we move the feeders from tree to tree so that the goldfinches are always set off by the flowers. It is a dazzling sight to behold, like a lovely Japanese print.

A number of years ago, there was a 6-inch snowfall toward the end of April. It was a freak storm and upset the recently arrived robins, for they were unable to search for worms, their favorite spring food. It was eerie, for scores of them huddled together on the porch that led to the back door. Usually, robins are not tame, and if a human being suddenly makes an appearance, they all fly off in panic. Phones were ringing all over the North Fork. Everybody was having the same experience. Friends from the Audubon Society advised us to put some ground hamburger out for the robins to eat. They picked at ours but preferred just sitting there, watching the storm from a sheltered point of view. Mercifully, the next morning, the temperature rose dramatically, all the snow melted, the robins went about digging their worms, and things were back to normal.

Our first spring spectacle is when the rock garden wakes up from its winter sleep. The very first plants to bloom, often occurring at the end of February, are the sturdy *Galanthus*, or snowdrops. They are not flamboyant plants but they naturalize readily and so after a few years, the spanking white, bell-like blossoms make a statement by sheer volume. They send their blossoms right up through the snow and bloom for about six weeks, welcoming the new spring season. When you see them bloom, you know that soon, not too soon, but soon, the dreary late-winter days will be over. At the same time, the green shoots of daffodils, tulips, crocus, and all the other bulbs begin to emerge from the frozen ground.

A true snowdrop spectacle is a rare thing, and I know of only one that I have ever heard of. There was a fine gentleman who lived in East Hampton, New York, a former American ambassador. He had a substantial house there and decided that he wanted to have a garden. So he planted a hundred thousand snowdrops on his property. Of course, it is a spectacle every spring. However, that is it. There are no flowering plants anywhere else on the grounds. There is nothing for midspring, late spring, summer, or fall. Only snowdrops.

By the end of March, when all else is bleak and dreary, when the trees have not yet leafed out, and when few other plants, shrubs, or flowering trees are in bloom, the rock garden is in full bloom. As soon as the rocks warm up just a bit from the late-winter sun, scores of beguiling little plants offer their sparkling blossoms.

Some people are fortunate in that their property is sloped or contains outcroppings of stones and boulders, but the landscape here on the North Fork of Long Island is flat, so when we installed our rock garden, we had to figure out how to make it appear natural, rather than superimposed on the flat landscape. We started by creating a 3- to 4-inch rise in the ground level at the back of the garden. Then we "planted" the rocks, that is, placed

them in the ground to make them look like a mountain or alpine landscape. If you decide to put in a rockery, never set rocks on top of the earth. They must be aesthetically placed with only the top or side parts exposed. The rest of the stone should be buried under the soil, as it is in nature.

When you design your rock garden, plan it so that it is easy to maintain. In areas without plants, add gravel scree, mulch, or spreading plants. Purists are very fussy about rock gardens and have rigid ideas about what they should look like. There are rules, and lots of them. In our garden, rules are made to be broken. Our rock garden is painterly; that is, we use drifts of color.

Beyond a selection of specimen plants and minor bulbs, we use low-growing plants that spread gently and cover bare

spaces. These include moss thyme, various sedums, *Echiveria* (hens and chicks), *Phlox subulata* (moss pink), ice plant, dwarf veronicas, draba, dianthus, arabis, and many others. A few hours of weeding every other week or so is all it takes to keep it looking tidy.

Rockeries adapt well to small properties. They can range in size from a very large gar-

Galanthus (snowdrops) are the first minor bulbs to bloom in the spring, often flowering in late January. ■ Perhaps now you can see why our rock garden is one of our favorites. Long before the rest of the garden wakes up, the rockery is in dazzling full bloom.

den to one only 12 by 12 feet, to even a tiny vest-pocket rock garden, or a trough garden, for that matter. A rockery can accommodate hundreds of different plants, allowing you considerable freedom in your design. Since alpine plants are almost always native to dry mountainous areas, they are tough, drought-resistant, and almost always free of pest or disease problems. If your time and space are limited, there is no better garden for you to enjoy.

The first rock gardens occurred naturally in landscapes where bare rock protrudes from the soil. Native plants filled the gaps with greenery, gardeners observed, and the alpine or rock garden was born. During the nineteenth-century era of horticultural exploration, these sparkling, intensely colored little gems of the plant world were collected and introduced. Botanists found them high in the Alps, Himalayas, Andes, and Rockies.

One plant that we grow is *Anemone pulsatilla* (European pasqueflower). It is early blooming with purple, red, or white blossoms, and its feathery foliage lasts throughout the season. Another, *Alyssum saxatile,* is a sprawling plant with gray leaves and masses of either sulfur yellow or cream blossoms in early spring. Dwarf columbines add a delicate touch. Dwarf spreading veronicas are low growing and are bright or pale blue, pink, or white. Dwarf dianthus, like 'Maiden Pink' or 'Scotch Pink,' add silver-blue foliage and charming clove-scented flowers to the garden. White arabis with its pale green-gray fuzzy foliage blooms for several months. There are also many different dwarf thymes, saponaria, sedums, violets, the stunning cushion-like aubrietas, white star-shaped arenaria, dwarf *Campanula carpatica,* and the dwarf *Iberis sempervirens* 'Little Gem' or candytuft.

Meanwhile, as the weeks pass, there are signs of spring everywhere. The Boston ivy on the stockade fence begins to leaf out. Pink *Clematis montana rubens* and white *Clematis montana wilsonii* begin to prepare for the midspring spectacle of a thousand blossoms. The native *Dodecatheon* (shooting star) is ready to bloom. Native mayapples and Solomon's seal poke through the ground in the woodland garden.

In our rock garden, we have also planted many minor bulbs. All are hardy as far north as Zone 3 and are planted in the fall. They thrive in full sun or partial shade, and often in deep shade. Since they are dormant in the summer, they are drought resistant. Of these, the standard Dutch crocus is probably the best known. But species crocus, less well known, bloom earlier and are far more versatile. Here is a list of some of the species crocus varieties. All grow to from 2 to 4 inches high.

Cherry red *Anemone pulsatilla* is one of our favorite alpine perennial plants. After bloom, the fluffy seedpods remain on the plant for months, and the feathery foliage stays green until a killing frost. ■ Here, early-blooming snowdrops are combined with mini-species crocus. They bloom together in February. This golden yellow variety is *Crocus ancyrensis,* 'Golden Bunch.'

VARIETY	COLOR
Crocus ancyrensis 'Golden Bunch'	Deep golden yellow
C. angustifolius (or *C. susianus*)	Bronze gold
C. chrysanthus 'Advance'	Outer petals purple, inner petals lemon yellow
C. chrysanthus 'Blue Bird'	Outer petals deep violet, inner petals white
C. chrysanthus 'Blue Pearl'	Delicate blue
C. chrysanthus 'Canary Bird'	Orange cup with bronze spots
C. chrysanthus 'Cream Beauty'	Cream white with dark markings
C. chrysanthus 'Snow Bunting'	White with gray and bronze-yellow center
C. sieberi 'Firefly'	Pale mineral-violet with yellow throat
C. sieberi 'Tricolor'	Lilac-blue with white band and yellow throat
C. sieberi 'Violet Queen'	Amethyst purple
C. tommasinianus 'Whitewell Purple'	Violet with white inner petals
C. tommasinianus 'Lady Killer'	Violet-purple with white margin
C. tommasinianus 'Ruby Giant'	Pale lavender with darker margin

Violet-scented purple *Iris reticulata* and species *Crocus chrysanthus* 'Snow Bunting' are certainly a wake-up call for early spring.

There are many other "minor" bulbs that have great charm that you should add to your spring garden:

Anemone blanda (Greek anemone) with bluish-purple, pink, red, or white daisy-like blossoms, medium green, leafy foliage, grows 4 to 6 inches high. Soak rhizomes in

Chionodoxa luciliae (glory-of-the-snow) has blue star-shaped blooms and spear-like foliage. They thrive in sun or shade and, given a few years, will completely cover the ground, surrounding large maple and beech trees with a carpet of lovely blue blossoms. ■ Blooming along with snowdrops are the buttercup-shaped *Eranthis* (winter aconite), a minor bulb that must be planted no later than August or it will not bloom the following year.

room-temperature water for forty-eight hours before planting. The white variety is particularly effective when interplanted with 'Red Riding Hood' tulips.

Chionodoxa luciliae (glory-of-the-snow) with blue, pink, or white star-shaped blooms, spear-like, medium green foliage grows 4 to 5 inches high. They are easy to grow and multiply readily into substantial clumps.

Eranthis hyemalis (winter aconite) with bright yellow, small, buttercup-like blossoms on 2- to 4-inch medium green clusters of foliage. Plant as soon as they are available in late summer. Soak in tepid water for twenty-four hours before planting. The most common cause of failure is late planting. The longer the tubers sit on shelves or in your house, the drier they get and the less likely they are to grow. Along with *Galanthus* (snowdrops), they are the earliest of all the spring-blooming bulbs, often growing right through the snow. And, if conditions are right, they will self-sow and naturalize.

Galanthus nivalis (snowdrop) have translucent white, bell-shaped blossoms and slender medium green foliage. Once planted, leave them where they are since each year the bloom display will become more and more lush and dramatic.

Iris danfordiae with bright yellow, iris-shaped blossoms are 6 inches high, with grass-like foliage. Although they rarely bloom a second year, these iris are worth the effort of planting every fall. Along with the *Iris reticulata,* they provide sparkling, late-winter color in a country garden.

Iris reticulata with light blue, lavender, or purple iris-shaped blooms are 6 inches high with grass-like foliage. This low-growing iris often blooms as early as late February. Coupled with *Iris danfordiae*'s bright yellow blossoms, they certainly lift the late-winter doldrums.

Puschkinia scilloides (striped squill) have bluish white or white clusters of ½- to 1-inch blossoms on 4- to 8-inch stalks over strap-like foliage. Like *Chionodoxa*, a fine companion plant, it will self-sow and naturalize if conditions are favorable. A bulb that should be more popular, *Puschkinia* is ideal for the spring rock garden, tucked here and there in the front of the border, or by the dooryard.

Scilla (squill) offers brilliant electric blue, pale blue, lilac, pink, or white bell-shaped or star-shaped blossoms on 3- to 12-inch stems over strap-like leaves. With its sensationally beautiful electric blue blossoms, *Scilla sibirica* is perhaps our favorite early spring-blooming minor bulb. The blossoms of *Scilla tubergeniana* are pale blue or white and, although charming, do not have the visual impact of the *sibirica*s.

Tulipa species are utterly charming dwarf tulips that originate in the wild. There are scores of varieties of them, and they are a fine addition to all early-spring gardens. They are well suited to the rock garden or tucked here and there near entrances or within view of windows so that they can be enjoyed during the late-winter and early-spring days. Species tulips come in many colors, including yellow, white, red, bronze, blue, rose, purple, or combinations thereof. The blossoms are usually 1 to 2 inches in diameter and are tulip-shaped at the top of erect 3- to 18-inch stems over broad, medium green foliage, some twisted. If these irresistible early-blooming miniature tulips are happy, they will multiply as they do in nature. Here is a list of so-called wild species tulips for you to choose from:

VARIETY	COLOR	HEIGHT
Tulipa bakeri 'Lilac Wonder'	Lilac and yellow	12"
T. batalinii 'Apricot Jewel'	Deep apricot-orange	6"
T. batalinii 'Bright Gem'	Sulfur yellow	6"
T. batalinii 'Bronze Charm'	Yellow with bronze feathering	6"
T. batalinii 'Red Gem'	Vermilion red and azalea pink	6"
T. batalinii 'Yellow Jewel'	Bright yellow with rose	6"
T. biflora	Yellow and white	8"
T. clusiana 'Lady Jane'	Rose and white	8"
T. dasystemon	Yellow and white	3–6"
T. hageri 'Splendens'	Deep red	6"
T. humilis alba coerulea oculata	White with blue base	5"
T. humilis 'Eastern Star'	Bronze green	6"
T. humilis 'Persian Pearl'	Magenta rose	5"
T. praestans 'Fuselier'	Bright red bouquets	8–12"
T. saxatilis	Rose lilac	6"
T. turkestanica	White with yellow center	8"

T. kaufmanniana (water-lily tulips) are another variety of species tulips that also are low-growers and a good choice for early-spring gardens. And they tend to perennialize, repeating their display year in and year out. They come in many colors and combinations including salmon, scarlet, yellow, cream, apricot, and orange with their water-lily shaped blossoms erect on 6- to 12-inch stems over medium green, medium green and burgundy, or medium green and white foliage. Their blossoms are considerably larger than most of the species tulips. Here is a list of some that are readily available:

The charming species tulip *T. bakeri* 'Lilac Wonder' grows to only 6 inches. They bloom in early spring, way ahead of the more popular and well-known Darwin tulips. We grow them in the rock garden along with a dozen other varieties of these mini-jewels. ■ Bright yellow *Iris danfordiae*, another very early bulb, often poke their heads up through the snow.

VARIETY	COLOR	HEIGHT
Ancilla	Pink and white	6"
Chopin	Lemon yellow	6"
Fritz Kreisler	Salmon pink	6"
Gaiety	Rosy red	8"
Gold Coin	Scarlet-edged yellow	6–8"
Heart's Delight	Carmine and rose	10"
Kaufmanniana	Cream with yellow center	6"
Shakespeare	Salmon-orange-apricot	6–8"
Show Winner	Scarlet	6–8"
Stresa	Gold with orange border	7"
Vivaldi	Yellow and crimson	7"
Water lily	Cream and carmine	7"

The most popular of all the early-blooming Emperor tulips is the red variety, usually the first standard-sized tulip to bloom in the spring.

Both early and midseason tulips bloom in tandem with daffodils. But if you plant late-bloomers, like Darwin and lily-shaped tulips, the daffodils will be finished before the tulips bloom.

T. fosteriana (Emperor tulips) are early-blooming, tall tulips that tend to perennialize and provide a glimpse of the later spring glories of tulip bloom. You see them in gardens in early spring, often when snow is still on the ground. Because they grow 16 to 20 inches high, they are not particularly suitable for rock gardens, but they add early-spring splashes of color throughout the rest of the garden. Until recently only solid colors were available, but each year hybridizers are creating new and interesting varieties. The 4-inch turban-

shaped blossoms come in red, pink, yellow, white, orange, and combinations thereof. Foliage is medium green or medium green and purple. Emperors can also be used in a naturalized, woodland setting. Here are some varieties for you to select from:

VARIETY	COLOR
Flaming Purissima	Pale ivory, yellow, and rose
Humoresque	Carmine red petals with white edges
Orange Emperor	Buttery orange
Pink Emperor	Pale pink with a yellow base
Red Emperor	Fiery red with a yellow heart
Sweetheart	Yellow-edged white
White Emperor	Milky white
Yellow Purissima	Canary yellow

Here is a list of the minor, early spring bulbs in the order of sequence of bloom:

VARIETY	BLOOM TIME
Chionodoxa (glory-of-the-snow)	Early spring
Crocus (Dutch)	Late winter/early spring
Crocus (Species)	Late winter/early spring
Eranthis (winter aconite)	Late winter
Galanthus (snowdrop)	Late winter/early spring
Iris danfordiae	Late winter/early spring
I. reticulata	Late winter/early spring
Puschkinia	Early spring
Scilla siberica (squill)	Early spring
S. tubergeniana (squill)	Early spring
Tulipa fosteriana (Emperor tulip)	Early/midspring
T. kaufmanniana (water-lily tulip)	Early/midspring
T. species	Early/midspring

The green shoots of many bulbs start growing in January, and many people think that the bloom of the plant will be affected by very cold weather. Not so. Both bulbs and foliage are hardy, and in most cases, the blossoms will not be harmed by a late snow. All of the spring-blooming bulbs are planted in the fall for spring bloom, so be sure to check the mail-order sources and local nurseries for bulbs at that time of year.

Watch all bulb plantings carefully for rabbit damage. Rabbits love to eat the fresh green shoots of almost all bulbs except daffodils, squill, and hyacinths. Tulips and crocus are their favorites. If given the chance, they will chew them right down to the ground. After every rain or snow, sprinkle the plantings with dried blood, available at garden centers and nurseries. If this doesn't work, lay chicken wire over the entire planting. This will allow the shoots to emerge and grow and yet deter the rabbits, since they don't like stepping on chicken wire. Once tulips are about 6 to 8 inches tall, and the crocus begins to bloom, carefully remove the chicken wire, since the rabbits do not seem to like the more mature foliage. Although we don't like the rabbits to eat the young bulb shoots, we do like having a few of them around. And later in the season they choose to raise their young in the rock garden, which is always a treat to watch. The only time we ever had a deer on the property was about ten years ago, before we fenced in the garden. The mother was close by watching her baby fawn nibbling at the costmary.

There are many low-growing dwarf evergreens that add a structural and textural interest to a rock garden. They have needle-like foliage and come in a wide range of colors: blue, silver-blue, yellow, variegated yellow and white, and the entire range of green. Some are shaped like obelisks, some globular, some conical, and others spreading. There are also many small ferns, such as Japanese painted fern, and dwarf grasses, such as blood grass and dwarf blue fescue, that also add textural interest to a rock garden.

Once the flamboyant spring bloom is over, there are other alpine plants that fill the gap, but most rock garden enthusiasts plant dwarf annuals to provide color during the long summer and fall. With proper planning and plant selection, you can have color throughout the season, including winter. Many alpine plants have evergreen foliage in red, silver, purple, green, blue, or yellow.

One final word of warning to would-be alpine garden enthusiasts. Our addiction to the charm and romance of rockery plants has brought out our acquisitive nature. Somehow or other, we cannot resist adding this or that plant from the Andes, Himalayas, Alps, or tundra areas to the collection. Mercifully, the addiction is not expensive since most plants suitable for rockeries cost only a few dollars. And our cockapoo, Mr. Chips, has always been quite territorial about the rock garden. It is his world, and because it is on a small scale, he seems to feel very comfortable exploring there and enjoying the sun.

During the month of April, about five years after we had installed the rock garden and it had grown to maturity, the garden editor of a national magazine called and asked if we would do a story for them on installing a water garden. Needless to say, we were overjoyed at the idea, and of course said yes, we would. Now the question was where would we put the water garden. At first we thought it should be near the porch so that we could look out over it while we were having drinks or dinner. However, we soon realized that during the summer, when we do entertain outside, it was always out in the back area of the garden next to the rock garden. Further, the rock garden was already a very natural-looking mountain area. So we decided to add the water garden to the rock garden, thus creating a mountain stream and pond environment.

The upper part of our water garden includes three very gentle cataracts. We integrated this feature into the existing rock garden and continued the plantings of early-blooming alpine plants and miniature bulbs.

We contacted our friend Ken Ruzicka, who is one of the best water-garden designers we have ever met, and told him what we were doing. He kindly offered his help and experience to us. One of the first things he said to us was, "Remember, you are making a water garden, not a water park!" In other words, subtlety is the key. We have seen extravagant water gardens with enormous waterfalls, à la Yosemite Falls at Yosemite National Park, others with more cataracts than the Boboli Gardens in Italy, and others that bore a resemblance to the gardens at Versailles. There is so much water falling, bubbling, and gurgling that you can't hear yourself think. And all on a totally inappropriate scale to the size of the gardens. That made sense to us, and so Ken proceeded to design and install an intimate and breathtakingly beautiful water garden for us.

You can imagine our excitement the day he arrived with several helpers to start digging up the area next to the rock garden. But it was coupled with apprehension. As the years went by, we had grown very territorial about our rock garden. And now, here they were digging a hole that was to be 4 feet deep at the deepest end to assure that the fish, who would soon call it home, would have a protected place to go in the winter. And the rest of the pond had to have shelves, step-like levels, upon which various water plants would ultimately be placed.

Ken respected the layout and landscape of our rock garden and designed a small foot-and-a-half-high waterfall that appeared to emerge from the top of the garden. The water gently cascaded down through three 2- to 4-inch-high falls into the 4-foot-by-10-foot upper pond. At the foot of the pond was a large flat stone under which the water ran, then gently cascaded into the main pond below, which is about 12 feet in diameter. After the digging, the

Left: Here is a view of the water-falls and rock garden from a differ-ent perspective. *Middle:* In this view of the garden, St. Francis looks down over the *Iberis* (candy-tuft), perhaps in search of a hun-gry bird to feed. ▬ *Right:* From this vantage point, you can see how the waterfalls lead first to a small upper pond and then to the main lower pond where all of the fish and frogs live.

entire area was covered with a heavy-duty rubber liner. Then several tons of river stones and flat rocks were used to build the cataract area and to line the pond. Other stones were used to create paths in and around the garden and to create low retaining walls beyond the garden.

The genius of Ken's design is that this water garden environment looks totally natural and blends perfectly with the rock garden. Through the years, many visitors have said, "You are so fortunate to have a little brook running through your property." In addition, he designed the garden so that you are invited to walk into it and through it, so that you become part of the environment. Most water gardens that we have seen do not offer this participation. You stand on the outside of the pond and look in. Period! We have even placed a small marble bench behind the water garden so that when you walk through you can sit and look at the garden from within.

Preliminary plantings around the pond were installed, including dwarf conifers, some deciduous shrubs, grasses, Siberian and Japanese iris, and other perennials. Then the hose was placed in the bottom and turned on. Two days later the pond was filled with water. The pump was installed, turned on, and the water started cascading down the first cataract, then the second, third, and fourth, and finally into the upper and then into the main pond. We were utterly thrilled and overjoyed. It was wonderful! And it has come to be the most beau-tiful area of the garden. We spend every leisure hour there during the summers. We must admit, if offered the option, we would opt for the water garden over a swimming pool any day, for it offers priceless peace and solitude.

Snails were added to keep the sides of the pond clean, and then finally, the fish. I always tell people that there are goldfish, koi, smoked salmon, and filet of sole in the pond. Later, we added tadpoles or pollywogs, which have grown into fine-sized frogs. In the spring they chirp and during the summer they croak. It took only one day for the water spiders to arrive. These are harmless arachnids that wander around on the surface of water. I hadn't seen them since I was a child growing up in a swamp and brook-laced area of northern New Jersey.

Alien visitors who have shown up at our pond through the years include an errant mallard duck who stayed for a few days. Another time, the biggest blue heron in the entire world put down briefly. They do that and eat all the fish in the pond if given the chance. But luckily, we saw him and flayed our arms vigorously to frighten him away. Since the pond is shaded by nearby trees, and not too visible from above, it is only in the winter, when they have a good view of it, that the herons visit. But we keep the pond netted in the winter to keep both debris and herons out. Another time, a snake decided to curl up on one of the warm stones. Although he was harmless to people, I soon learned by watching him wiggle his way through the water in pursuit of a free meal that he had a hankering for tad-

The dwarf and miniature iris, and *Bergenia*, which thrives in a wet area, are in bloom around the banks of the lower pond. A water garden opens up an entire new world of plants to the gardener. Called "bog" plants, they thrive in muddy conditions.

poles and small fish. So, we threw a very large beach towel on him, wrapped him up and drove him about a half mile away to a creek, and let him go. Next day he was back. At least, we think it was the same snake. We recaptured him and drove him four miles away to a wetland area and let him go there. He has not returned.

As the weeks went by, the pond offered more and more diversion. We learned that fish can be hand-fed. You simply put the food in your hand, lower it near the water, and they all come and nibble at your palms while they eat their food. It tickles! And, being an amateur ornithologist, the most wonderful surprise for me was that many migratory and summer resident birds were attracted to the garden by the splashing of the waterfalls. One rarely sees these birds close up or at feeders. We have clocked several pairs of Baltimore orioles and orchard orioles. There are the usual blue jays, cardinals, goldfinches, titmice, chickadees, robins, redwings, and catbirds, but also yellow warblers, golden-throated warblers, yellow-throats, blackburnian and magnolia warblers, great-crested flycatchers, indigo buntings, rose-breasted grosbeaks, a scarlet tanager, summer tanagers, a blue grosbeak, and others too numerous to mention. They seem to come for their daily splash in late afternoon or early evening. And, at times, when a number of different colored birds are there at once, it is truly a breathtaking sight.

While our rock garden and water garden are in the first flush of spring, the rest of the garden is just beginning to show signs of life. The trees are still gaunt and leafless, autumn leaves litter the wooded areas waiting to be raked up and carted away, skies remain leaden, late snowfalls periodically interrupt the progress of spring, and cold rain and wind make the outdoors inhospitable to leisurely strolling through the garden.

But the coming of spring events continues relentlessly. Soon other spectacles will unfold. Already the creeping myrtle has put forth its star-shaped periwinkle blue blossoms. Throughout the garden, the primroses (*Primula vulgaris*) sport their spring yellow, sweet woodruff is beginning to show green, and here and there drifts of species and Dutch crocus, the little jewels of spring, dazzle with their brilliant color. But you need a fix of riotous color for a spectacular early-spring garden, and here is what we have done. Almost all gardeners know that the May garden, with its extravagant displays of dogwood, azaleas, rhododendrons, tulips, etc., is a knockout. In fact, I have often said you have to be a real ninny not to have a glorious garden in May. But in April, it is not so easy to achieve. Your choice of blooming plants is much more limited, and far less well known, than those that bloom later.

Through the years, we have pored over catalogues and books and kept notes about gardens that we saw during this time of year to find out what is in bloom and when, and usu-

This is Mr. Chips, our pet cocka-poo, up on a pedestal as usual. He loves to romp in the garden, chase rabbits, bury his biscuits in the rock garden, and pick his own tomatoes off the vines in summer.

ally found the plants we liked somewhere and installed them in the garden. Daffodils are pretty surefire when it comes to a spectacle and April is the time that they bloom. And so I began to dig up daffodils from my parents' place in New Jersey, divide them, and plant them in our woodland area. Each year I would buy more and plant them, bright yellow, white, orange, pink, bicolor, trumpets, large-cupped, doubles, tarzettas, standard, medium height, and the irresistible dwarfs, some of which grow to only 4 inches high. They are easy to plant and instructions are on every package that you buy. It is difficult to make a mistake in planting them.

Narcissus (daffodils) are tough plants, and rodents and deer loathe them. There are no pests or diseases that attack them. A little fertilizer each year helps them bloom, but even if you forget to add it, they still bloom their heads off. Their foliage dries in June and then disappears, and they go into dormancy. This means you don't have to worry about watering them during summer droughts. They are close to being the easiest of all plants to grow. Their scent is irresistible, bouquets brighten up the indoors, and mass plantings lift the spirits during the last dreary days of the winter–early spring season. Buy as many as you have the budget and time for and plant them in the fall.

All daffodils are reasonable in price and a joy to behold in spring. Despite the hundreds of varieties available, our favorites are still the miniatures, pink tones, and the stately bright yellow trumpet varieties. We have found that these less popular miniature daffodils add irresistible charm to dooryard gardens, rockeries, and foundation plantings. Still, many gardeners have not yet discovered them. These miniature daffodils are true bulbs and are available in yellow, orange, or white, and combinations thereof. The blossoms are trumpet-shaped or double on 4- to 14-inch stalks, depending on the variety, over medium green, spear-like foliage.

Select your varieties of *Narcissus* in the fall and plant them at a depth three times the diameter of the bulbs, about 2 to 6 inches apart. They prefer well-drained, ordinary soil, fortified with sphagnum peat moss and well-rotted compost or manure. Like all daffodils, miniature varieties are not fussy about soil or light, thriving in full sun or partial shade. Be sure to let the foliage brown naturally, and do not remove it until it is completely withered. The reason for this is that food and energy for next year's growth and flowers is restored through the leaves, and once the leaves have withered, the bulb is ready for next year's bloom. Here is a list of some of the varieties that we like:

Behind our little barn, we have a woodland garden. In April, year in and year out, the daffodils make a spectacle of themselves. The purple rhododendron is the early-blooming 'PJM,' a godsend to the early-spring garden. ■ Here is another view of our woodland garden. Both yellow forsythia and *Rhododendron* 'Cornell Pink' add the important dimension of height.

VARIETY	COLOR	HEIGHT
April Tears	Deep yellow	6–8"
Baby Moon	Buttercup yellow	9"
Double Jonquil	Double, bright yellow	10"
February Gold	Bright yellow and lemon	8"
Gold Drops	Yellow and white	10"
Hawera	Creamy yellow	8"
Hoop Petticoat	Bright yellow	6"
Jack Snipe	White and yellow	8"
Liberty Bells	Clusters of yellow	8"
Lintie	Yellow with orange rim	9"
Little Witch	Deep yellow	6"
Peeping Tom	Golden yellow	8"
Pipit	Sulphur and white	9"
Rip van Winkle	Double, clear yellow	6"
Suzy	Yellow and orange	14"
Tête-à-Tête	Yellow	8"

Daffodils are naturalized in a field adjoining the living area of the garden. They are so versatile and so easy to grow, thriving in almost any kind of environment. And neither rabbits nor deer can stand them. ■ What a picture! White 'Thalia' narcissus and pink *Dicentra* (bleeding heart) set off this white birch spectacularly.

Standard daffodils grow from 1½ to 2 feet tall, depending on the variety. There are eleven basic types, including the familiar trumpet, small-cupped, large-cupped, and so forth. All grow on erect stems over sword-like, medium green foliage. We have found that the double daffodils, which are quite spectacular, do not hold up well during spring rains, and almost every year end up mud-splattered with broken stems on the ground. Like their mini sisters, standard-sized daffodils prefer well-drained, ordinary soil, fortified with sphagnum peat moss and well-rotted compost or manure. They thrive in full sun or partial shade and are dormant in the summer. Plant in fall, to a depth of about three times the diameter of the bulb, 6 to 8 inches apart, depending on bulb size. As above, do not remove foliage until completely withered and brown.

Miniature daffodil, 'Rip van Winkle' and early-blooming, low-growing species *gregii* tulips are perfect additions to the rock garden.

Most varieties of daffodils perform well over a period of five, ten, or even fifteen to twenty years, though some do not. After the first three years, some form thick clumps of foliage, but steadily produce fewer flowers. In some instances the bulbs die out completely. Remember that if after a few years bloom becomes sparse, bulbs have multiplied to the point that they need dividing. After foliage has withered and dried, dig up the bulbs, separate, and either replant or store for the summer in an airy, shady place and plant in the fall. Each spring when shoots emerge, scratch in one tablespoon of 9-9-6 fertilizer per square foot of planting area.

Several years ago, at the Planting Fields Arboretum on Long Island, a daffodil-planting trial was installed in which two hundred different varieties of daffodils representing twenty classifications were planted in groups of six bulbs each. They were left undisturbed, and the number of flowers produced was tabulated each year. After ten years, some varieties were strong and still flowering to perfection. Others had fewer flowers, while still others had disappeared completely. The varieties that consistently produced a lavish display were:

VARIETY	COLOR	HEIGHT
Arctic Gold	Yellow	18"
Binkie	Yellow and white	12"
Campanile	Yellow and orange	14"
Carlton	Yellow	18"
Cherie	White and pink	12"

VARIETY	COLOR	HEIGHT
Dove Wings	Yellow with yellow	8"
Duke of Windsor	White and yellow-orange	18"
February Gold	Bright yellow and yellow	10"
Flower Record	White and white-orange	18"
Ice Follies	White with pale yellow	18"
March Sunshine	Yellow	9"
Mrs. R. O. Backhouse	White and pink	18"
Red Rascal	Yellow and red	18"
Spellbinder	Yellow and white	20"
Sweetness	Yellow	12"
Sun Chariot	Yellow and orange	20"
Thalia	Pure white	15"
Trevithian	Yellow	18"

Daffodil varieties that consistently produced a lavish display in the Netherlands Bulb Industry's four-year trials conducted at North Carolina State University included the following:

VARIETY	COLOR	HEIGHT
Barrett Browning	White and deep orange-red	20"
Brighton	Yellow	20"
Carbineer	Yellow and orange	18"
February Gold	Bright yellow and yellow	10"
Flower Record	White and white-orange	18"
Fortune	Yellow and orange	18"
Gigantic Star	Yellow	18"
Ice Follies	White with pale yellow	18"
Jumblie	Yellow and orange	9"
Salome	White and apricot-orange	15"
Sugarbush	White and yellow	12"
Tahiti	Yellow and orange-red	18"
Thalia	Pure white	15"
Trevithian	Yellow	18"

You can't have enough white 'Thalia' narcissus. They accent and combine well with perennials, shrubs, dwarf conifers, and flowering trees. ■ Native *Mertensia* (Virginia bluebells) and *Leucojum* are combined with pink hyacinths in our woodland garden. We feel that hyacinths are too stiff and formal for most gardens, but after they have been in the ground for several years, they loosen up and have a very nice wild, informal look about them.

By now, we have thousands of daffodils all over the garden and when in bloom the garden looks like a giant brass ensemble, playing a concerto to spring. Most are planted in a naturalized manner in what we call the woodland garden, a shaded area that we have left natural, not only for the informal, casual look that it has but also to save on maintenance and time. A simple little path runs through the area. We have added many plants, mostly native, including clear blue Virginia bluebells; tall, willowy Solomon's seal; purple and white violets; jack-in-the-pulpit; mayapples; graceful, pink bleeding hearts; purple-blue columbines; and feathery lavender *Thalicritum* (meadow rue). Bright green sweet woodruff, with its scented white blossoms, from which May wine is made, multiplies readily and serves as a fine ground cover. There are polka dot–leafed pulmonarias, with their nodding clusters of blue, white, or pink blossoms that have slowly grown into a lovely ground cover. *Helleborus orientalis* (lenten rose), with its rich brown-purple-rose, white-spotted bloom, is always a welcome spring sight as is *Petasites fragrans* (Japanese butterbur), a compact, spreading evergreen perennial that sports small purple to white, vanilla-scented flowers.

Here is a list of midseason bulbs:

Convallaria majalis (**lily of the valley**)

Fritillaria meleagris

F. michailovskyi

F. persica

F. imperialis

Muscari (**grape hyacinth**)

Narcissus (**standard daffodil**)

Triumph tulip

Double or peony tulip

Darwin hybrid tulip

Tulipa gregii

Scilla campanulata (**squill**)

We have never included tulips in our daffodil planting; however, there are several divisions of early tulips that do bloom in tandem with daffodils, and we have them in other parts of the garden. They are *T. fosteriana* or Emperor tulips and the dwarf *T. gregii*.

T. gregii are midseason bloomers quite similar to *T. kaufmannianas*, but bloom somewhat later and are a bit larger. Perhaps the best known is 'Red Riding Hood,' which grows to only 6 inches and is a good addition to a rock garden for it offers brilliant red color after

Here is another view of our naturalized woodland garden. Daffodils are at their peak here, and early-blooming rhododendrons and azaleas complement the planting nicely.
■ A rainbow of tulips is planted beneath this spring-blooming apple tree and the rhododendron.

the earlier tulips have bloomed and it tends to bloom for many years. The tulip-shaped or water lily–shaped blooms of *gregii*s are on 6- to 20-inch erect stems over medium green foliage, usually mottled with purple or brown. The colors are orange, red, yellow, cream, pink, ivory, and combinations thereof. Here are some varieties you might like:

VARIETY	COLOR	HEIGHT
Calypso	Red with yellow margins	12"
Corsage	Rose, edged yellow	10–12"
Donna Bella	Carmine red with cream edges	12"
Elise	Creamy yellow tinted with pink	8"
Oratorio	Apricot-rose	8"
Pinocchio	Scarlet red with yellow	10"
Quebec	Rose-red with cream	14"
Red Riding Hood	Carmine red with black	6"
Royal Splendour	Vermillion red	20"
Toronto	Tangerine red	14"
Tsar Peter	Sulfur white with rose	10"

There are a number of other varieties of tulips that bloom in mid-spring. The following usually bloom after the daffodils and early spring flowers and shrubs are finished but before the glorious May display of azaleas, dogwoods, and rhododendrons. They are Triumph tulips, double or peony-flowered tulips, and Darwin hybrid tulips. The best known of the Triumph tulips is 'Apricot Beauty,' a true apricot-colored tulip that tends to perennialize. It grows to about 18 inches and is a welcome sight after the early tulips have finished their bloom cycle. 'Angelique,' a lovely pale pink and white fluffy tulip, is the most popular of the double or peony-flowered tulips. We have had some that perennialized and are now in their fifth year. The Darwin hybrids are the tallest and most majestic of all tulips, some growing to 2½ feet high. They are very flamboyant in color, are very reliable, come in a large range of colors, and are the most likely tulips of all to perennialize. We have one that goes back twenty years and is in a totally wrong place, but since it has persisted so long, we just leave it there and enjoy it every year.

In Europe, tulips are treated as annuals. They are planted in the fall and then after they bloom, they are dug up and discarded. Most tulips do not perennialize, and the bulbs get smaller and smaller each year, eventually ceasing to bloom or dying. The Netherlands Bulb Industry has run trial plantings of specific varieties of tulips for four years in conjunction with North Carolina State University to test their tendency to perennialize. The varieties that performed best are listed below. Some are readily available from suppliers; others are not so easy to locate. I suggest you refer to the bulb source list, send for a dozen or so catalogues, go through them, and select from the recommended lists.

The trials run by North Carolina State University were planted in zones 7, 8, and 9, among the milder climatic regions of the country. This does not necessarily mean that these tulip varieties will not do as well in cooler zones. However, be advised that similar results in your garden, no matter where it is, are most assuredly not guaranteed. And although some Darwin, Triumph, Parrot, and double early tulips received high ratings for perennialization, the majority of those with high ratings were the Darwin hybrids.

Here is a list of midseason tulips that may perennialize:

VARIETY	COLOR
Candela	Yellow
Diplomat	Red
Frankfurt	Red
Golden Apeldoorn	Yellow
Golden Oxford	Yellow
Golden Parade	Yellow
Gudoshink	Yellow, fringed with orange
Hoango	Yellow
Ile de France	Red
Jewel of Spring	Yellow, edged red
Los Angeles	Red, edged yellow
Merry Widow	Red, edged white
Monte Carlo	Yellow
Negrita	Purple
Orange Emperor	Orange
Oscar	Red
Oxford	Red
Princess Victoria	Red, edged white
Spring Song	Red, edged white

VARIETY	COLOR
Striped Apeldoorn	Yellow, striped red
Yellow Dover	Yellow
Yokohama	Yellow, edged red

There are a number of other minor bulbs that you might want to include in your mid-spring plantings. Some will blend quite well with daffodils:

Fritillaria imperialis (crown imperial) sport red, orange, or yellow clusters of bell-shaped blossoms on erect clusters of 3- to 4-inch-high stems. The blossoms do not smell pleasant so they are best kept away from dooryards or windows. All animals hate them.

F. meleagris (guinea-hen flower) have purple and white or white drooping, bell-shaped blossoms with a checkered pattern over grass-like, 12-inch-high foliage. Plants often naturalize once established.

F. michailovskyi (Michael's flower) has very interesting bell-shaped blossoms in a bronze-maroon edged in yellow on strap-like, 8- to 12-inch foliage.

F. persica (Persian bells) sport mysterious deep purple-violet bell-shaped blossoms that are very fragrant. They look like flowers that Vincent Price might have used to poison his wife. Strap-like foliage stands 3 feet high. These are particularly effective in the garden when set off by yellow and white daffodils.

Hyacinthus orientalis (Dutch hyacinth) are the familiar blue-purple, red, pink, yellow, cream, white, or orange columnar spikes of flowerlets. Their foliage is jade green, strap-like and from 8 to 12 inches high. They are easy to grow but we find that their stiff appearance makes it difficult to use them effectively in our landscape. However, after the first year of bloom, the stalks of flowerlets loosen up substantially, taking on a lovely, informal look. Their scent is unforgettable.

Muscari (grape hyacinth) is now available in many new forms. The colors may be bright blue, pale blue, violet, purple, white, or combinations thereof. They bloom over sprawling, strap-like, foliage from 4 to 12 inches high. Most of these cultivars sport flowers that resemble bunches of grapes. They perfume the surrounding air with a subtle, sweet fragrance. They are particularly effective when planted as an undercover for daffodils. We were very happy to see, and now grow, the new *Muscari* 'Valerie Finnis.' Several years ago, we were in England on assignment, doing a story on Sir David Montague Scott and Lady Scott's garden at the Dower House at Boughton Hall in Northamptonshire.

Deep blue *Muscari* (grape hyacinth), which combines so very well with yellow daffodils, can also serve as a foreground for tulips. In this case, yellow Darwin and red lily-flowering tulips. ■ One of the most popular of all tulips is this pastel pink 'Angelique' peony-flowering variety, planted in a lovely drift with *Muscari* in the foreground.

Lady Scott is also known as Valerie Finnis, the garden photographer and writer. We had a fine visit, became friends, and Sir David invited us to come to his hundredth birthday party, which was to be held about six months later. Unfortunately, he died shortly after our visit at the age of ninety-nine. He never did live to see a hundred and that star-studded birthday party he had planned, with everyone who was anyone in attendance, including his cousin the queen. We wanted to make some sort of gesture, so we picked some of our roses, dried the petals, and sent them to Lady Scott so that she could scatter them throughout Sir David's beautiful garden. But since we were the last friends of the many that he had made on this earth, she chose to put them in the stone memorial that she had placed in the garden that contained some of his most cherished things.

Here are some available varieties of grape hyacinths:

VARIETY	COLOR	HEIGHT
Muscari armeniacum	Blue clusters	4–8"
M. armeniacum 'Cantab'	Cambridge blue	4–8"
M. armeniacum 'Christmas Pearl'	Violet-blue	6"
M. armeniacum 'Saffier'	Deep French blue	8"
M. aucheri 'Blue Magic'	Sky blue with white eyes	6–8"
M. botryoides 'Album'	White clusters	4–8"
M. comosum 'Plumosum' (Feather)	Reddish-purple plumes	6–8"
M. hybrid 'Blue Spike'	Double blue clusters	10–12"
M. latifolium	Rich blue clusters	2–15"
M. neglectum	Blue, edged white	4–8"
M. paradoxum	Blue, edged black greenish-yellow	6–8"
M. 'Valerie Finnis'	Light blue with silver	6"

Every year, we also buy flats of pansies and fill up the window boxes, porch and patio planters, and urns with them. They are quite reasonable and add gleaming color to any garden in early spring. And this past year, we finally came up with a solution for planting salad greens and kitchen herbs. When the garden was young, we planted all manner of vegetables, the complete spectrum. But then as the years wore on and the garden became more and more complex, we simply didn't have the time for vegetables. Besides that, on the North Fork, the farmers grow very respectable vegetables and sell them at farm stands. And they are very reasonable in price. So we have decided to leave vegetables to them.

However, we still grow fresh herbs, spring salad greens, and tomatoes. We used to grow

We grow a spring crop of lettuce, interplanted with pansies, in planters right on the porch next to the kitchen door. Now we don't have to run all the way back to the South 40 to get some lettuce as the finishing touch on a platter of smoked salmon or, more likely, a ham and Swiss on rye.

them in the back garden. This was really quite impractical, and it took many years to come to this conclusion. When you are in the middle of making an omelet and you need chives or parsley, you never make the trek out to the back garden to pick it. We then moved greens and herbs up to a kitchen garden near the kitchen door. We tended to neglect them. So, we placed them in the planters right outside the door, mixed first with pansies and then with petunias. And we enjoyed sweet lettuce, arugula, mustard, and cress all spring, and fresh herbs all season long. Since our summering houseplants are in that area, we never forgot to water or feed them. It was a splendid solution.

When I first moved out here, "somewhere in the Mid-Atlantic" according to my late father, people sold every conceivable thing at little tables or stands in front of their houses. Flowers, bread, vegetables, furniture, birdhouses, and crafts. One person had a collection of eight barber's chairs for sale, and another had six ancient cannons and cannonballs. After a few years, I had quite a stand of daffodils, and thought I might try putting some out in front of the house to see if they would sell. I spoke with Miss Hazel King, my neighbor across the street about it. Miss King, and I never called her Hazel, ultimately lived to be 105 years old, passing away only a few years ago. Her grandfather and her father had farmed the land across the street from me since before 1840. She had gone to a fancy New England boarding school, made the "Grand Tour" in 1908, had studied dance with Isadora Duncan, and one of her old beaus was the poet Archibald MacLeish. In the 1990s, when she died, there were still people out here who thought of her as a "newbie."

Coming from Yankee stock, she told me that she thought that selling daffodils was a good idea, and that I would probably make some money at it. Then she added, "But don't put limas out. There's no money in limas." So I made a sign that read DAFFS—3$ A BUNCH, picked six bouquets of daffodils, and put them in mayonnaise jars, which I then placed in a milk crate on a table. A peanut jar was there for the money. That's the way it was done out here. Nobody even thought twice about it. I set up my stand and then went inside the house to work. About an hour later, my late basset hound, William (a.k.a. Akerwood Findlay), was at the living room window, barking his head off. I went in and peeked out behind the curtain and saw that all of my daffodils were gone. I thought, "It took only one hour for someone to rip me off." Then I looked more carefully and saw money in the peanut butter jar. I went out and much to my astonishment found eighteen dollars in the jar. A lightbulb went on in my head, and I sold daffodils every year after that for almost fifteen years. It was fun, I met many people through my little business, and eventually, neighbors looked at it as a happy sign of spring.

In all those years, there was only one time that I was ripped off. It was about one o'clock in the afternoon. I was working in my office and the phone rang. It was Miss King.

She said, "There's a great big black limousine with smoked glass windows sitting in front of your daffodil stand! And a liveried chauffeur standing next to the car." I went to the window and pulled the curtains aside just a bit so that I could see it, and yes, it was there. The window rolled down and the chauffeur went to my stand, took one bunch of daffodils, and walked to the open window with it. A white-gloved hand appeared, took the bouquet, and the window was rolled up again. Then, for what seemed forever, the chauffeur waited. After a while, the window rolled down again and she gave him the money in her cupped hands to pay for the flowers. He put the money in the jar, went back to the car, and sped off down the road. Of course I immediately went outside to collect the money, and when I got there I discovered that she had paid in pennies, and shortchanged me thirteen cents, which, I suspect, is how the rich got rich and how the rich stay rich.

When I first moved into the house, Miss King was indeed suspicious of me. But we later became very close friends, to the point that she spent Thanksgiving, Christmas, and other holidays with us, as part of the family. Many years later I told her, "I bet you couldn't wait until that first Christmas to see if I put a wreath on the door to find out if I was a Christian or not."

"You bet," she quipped. When I first became friendly with her, she told me "You're smart to move out here!" I asked why and she said, "Because people live forever out here."

About five years after I bought the house, a few of the old outbuildings and a portion of the main house that remained of the old King farm down on the corner were for sale. My late father thought the little barn would be a fine addition and so gave it to me as a birthday gift. We moved it shortly after. When I told Miss King that we had bought her little barn and were going to move it here, she said, "It was not a barn, it was our carriage house, and it was built in 1812, the year Napoleon went to Russia." She also told me that there had been a six-holer Victorian-style outhouse on the property, but that it had been carted away many years before.

Soon after the daffodil plantings had become established, we realized that the backbone of the spring garden, that is, shrubs and flowering trees, had to be added. We did have several forsythia, indeed a cliché, but they do fill a need for about three weeks in early spring when they sport brilliant yellow or gold flowers. And, in most gardens, they are a welcome sight. In our garden, they complement the daffodils and other plantings. Our forsythia were the old-fashioned standard varieties, which were among the few plants here when I bought the house. They can grow to 12 feet and spread vigorously to the point that they are invasive. The weeping versions multiply by sending large branches that bend to the ground and then send out roots. We removed a number of them and pruned and divided others.

Even though this Korean rhododendron 'Cornell Pink' is in its first year, it already makes a statement in the woodland garden. You should see it now! It's over 6 feet tall with a cottony cloud of pink blossoms in April.

We have since learned that it is best for our garden and the size of our property to plant only the dwarf varieties of forsythia. You will have to shop around for them, but there are many available, and it is well worth the search. *Forsythia viridissima* 'Bronxensis' grows only to about 3 feet. *F.* x *intermedia* 'Minigold' grows to 4 to 5 feet. *F.* 'New Hampshire Gold' grows to 4 to 5 feet. They are all vigorous but must be well watered throughout the season for the first year until they are established. After that, they are quite maintenance free.

There are many early-blooming rhododendrons, some standard size, but mostly attractive dwarf plants. The *Rhododendron mucronulatum* (Korean rhododendron) is a fine complement to daffodils and forsythia, and we have opted for a variety called 'Cornell Pink' that blooms at the same time as the daffodils in a lovely soft pink color. We have added a half dozen to the landscape. We have also added about a dozen dwarf rhododendrons, including 'Baden-Baden,' a brilliant red pom-pom variety; 'Purple Gem,' a tough purple dwarf; the pastel yellow 'Princess Ann'; yellow 'Patty Bee'; and *R.* x *keiskei*. *R.* 'Black Satin' has deep green, almost black foliage, and *R. fastigatum* has mini, purple clusters of flowers. They are all elegant little plants and add a nice touch of class to the early spring garden.

Daphne 'Carol Mackie' and many other varieties bloom in early spring. We have *Erica* (Heath), with its little spikes of pink, white, or red flowers but find that their tiny, needle-like evergreen leaves often get to look quite raffish after a while. We heavily prune them every two years or so, practically down to 2 inches, to force new, orderly foliage. *Skimmia* is another spring-blooming shrub in our garden. This low-growing, elegant, broad-leafed evergreen offers clusters of white blossoms. Evergreen *Cotoneaster congestus* (Pyrenees cotoneaster) forms a dense mound with pink flowers and *Cotoneaster conspicuus decorus* (necklace cotoneaster) is a nice ground cover with white flowers in early spring and a bonus of profuse red berries in the fall. *Pieris japonica* (Japanese andromeda or lily of the valley shrub) is an imposing evergreen with pendulous clusters of creamy white flowers like those of lily of the valley. There are also several *Viburnum* that are great additions to our spring garden. The lovely scented *Viburnum* x *burkwoodii* (burkwood viburnum) is grown primarily for its early-spring, highly scented, pinkish-white blossoms, and *Virburnum rhytidophyllum* (leatherleaf viburnum) flowers in early spring with large, flat, yellowish-white clusters of blossoms.

Some plants begin to leaf out before others, so we have added them to the early-spring garden. We have six different varieties of Japanese maples, all dwarfs, growing only 4 to 6 feet. *Acer palmatum* 'Shaina' is a lovely greenish-red, others are lacy-leafed, deep red varieties, or yellow-green and green with yellow edges. Our *Cotinus coggygria* (smoke bush) offers deep purple-mahogany foliage and begins to leaf out at this time. These are large plants, some growing to 15 feet, so if you use them in a shrub border be sure to opt for the smaller variety, *C. coggygria* 'Pink Champagne,' which can be kept to 4 to 5 feet by pruning judiciously during the season. The deep purple foliage is a nice contrast to the usual sea of green seen in most gardens.

Early spring is also the time for magnolias. No, not the *Magnolia grandiflora* (Southern magnolia), for that blooms here in August, but the early spring-blooming *M. stellata* (star magnolia) and *M.* x *soulangiana* (saucer magnolia). We have three star magnolias in the garden. They are covered with 3- to 4-inch star-shaped white blossoms and are among the earliest of all flowering trees to bloom. Within a few weeks the stunning pink *M.* x *soulangiana* bloom. We have three of these and have recently added two of the startlingly beautiful yellow *M.* x *soulangiana* 'Elizabeth' and 'Butterflies.' They are very fast-growing trees and within five years or so stand about 15 to 20 feet high. Few gardeners know of these new yellow varieties. The story about how they came to be is an interesting one. Horticulturists at the Brooklyn Botanic Garden were experimenting with the *Magnolia* x *soulangiana* and planted hundreds of seeds from trees in their collection. One turned out to be a sport,

Looking toward the south façade of the house, the April garden is beginning to come into its own. On the right next to the little barn are two unusual evergreens. The tall one is a columnar boxwood, and the weeping plant next to it is a Sargent's weeping hemlock (*Tsuga canadensis* 'Pendula').

Left: One of the first small, flowering trees to bloom is the *Magnolia stellata* (star magnolia), with its fragrant star-shaped white blossoms. The yellow forsythia behind it offers a nice contrast of color. ▓ *Middle:* The pink magnolia 'Leonard Messel' is a variety of the *Magnolia stellata* and blooms at the same time. It is quite effective as a companion plant. ▓ *Right:* Our first pink *Camellia japonica* is now over 15 feet tall. The pink hyacinths and electric blue *Scilla siberica* make this planting quite special.

and, much to everyone's amazement, bloomed with yellow, saucer-shaped flowers. Up to that point, this cultivar was available only in pink or white and sometimes pale purple coloration. It was named 'Elizabeth.' Then, horticulturists began to hybridize other varieties from this one so that now there are more than ten different yellow magnolias. They are readily available now and are worth pursuing since they are utterly lovely when in bloom.

About fifteen years ago, we decided to experiment and plant camellias. Knowing that our area was in Zone 7A, I was sure that they would survive. Since the North Fork is surrounded by warming waters and the winter temperature almost never goes below 10 degrees in the winter, we began to think about planting cultivars that I had never seen in gardens in New Jersey when I was growing up. When we planted the first one, savvy gardener-neighbors called us city slickers, laughed, and said we were throwing our money away.

They were wrong. Fifteen years later that first camellia, a pink *Camellia japonica* is 15 feet tall and is covered with hundreds of blooms every April. We did make a mistake, however, when we planted it by putting it in a spot with a southern exposure. The blossoms do burn and brown slightly in the strong sunlight. The more recent additions are in shade or on an east or northern exposure so bloom does not burn. We now have five other japonicas in various parts of the garden. *C. sasanquas* are supposed to be even less hardy than the japonicas. We planted five of them, and they all are thriving. They bloom in November and December. One of the varieties, a white single named 'Snowflake,' sported at the National Arboretum, and we were very fortunate to be given one by a gardener friend. If you live in Zone 7A, be sure to plant some. If you are below Zone 7A, chances that they will survive the winter are very slim.

The last of the major shrub blooms of the early spring are the tree peonies. Unlike herbaceous peonies, the better-known varieties that die down to the ground in winter, tree peonies maintain their structure, usually about 4 feet high, with buds and blossoms emerging from the existing stems rather than sending up new growth each year. Their bloom is nothing short of spectacular, almost garish, but in early spring, they brighten the landscape like colorful beacons. There are hundreds to choose from with blossoms in red, yellow, purple, white, pink, and combinations thereof. Blossoms are 6 to 12 inches in diameter. Don't overlook them, and plant at least three of them in your garden since they are always a conversation piece. They like well-drained, moist, rich soil to which you add ample organic matter. They live for a very long time, so be sure to prepare the soil before planting. Tree peonies add great splashes of color wherever you might want or need it in the early-spring garden.

The late-spring and the May–June garden is the most spectacular of any during the growing season. Scores of perennials bloom along with dogwoods, azaleas, rhododendrons, lilacs, peonies, and iris all blooming one after the other throughout the garden. At this time of year, every day brings new bloom, often three, four, or five different cultivars opening on the same day. It is the most exciting and gratifying time in any gardener's year. Many consider the May-flowering tulips the most beautiful of all tulips. And if you plan your garden carefully, you can have many other plants blooming at the same time. Among these are the equally spectacular azaleas, dogwoods, and rhododendrons.

Although the early and midseason tulips either have finished blooming or are nearing the end of their cycle, the May-flowering tulips are just about to begin their annual spectacle. All of these are late-bloomers. You can never have too many in your garden so be reckless when you order your late-blooming tulips. As with all other tulips, they prefer well-drained, ordinary soil fortified with sphagnum peat moss, and will bloom in either full sun or partial shade. After bloom, the foliage will brown. When it does, then remove it, but not before it is brown and withered. Rabbits and other rodents love the tender shoots of tulips, so protect them by placing pieces of chicken wire over the planting. New shoots will

Here, the early May garden is at its peak. The yellow Darwin tulips planted throughout this part of the garden are especially appealing among the pink azaleas.

This pink Darwin tulip is called 'Menton' and is one of our favorites because it is almost the same color as some of the pink azaleas in the garden. We mix white and pale yellow tulips along with the pink 'Menton' in the azalea planting area.

grow through the holes in the chicken wire. When they are about 6 inches tall, carefully remove the chicken wire. Tulips are dormant in the summer so you need not worry about watering them during periods of drought. And they are pest and disease free. The following are the late bloomers:

Cottage and Darwin tulips are the most popular tulips of all, and always have been. They are the latest flowering tulips available and are the largest class, with the most diverse colors. They grow to about 2 feet. You can never have enough of them in your garden.

Fringed tulips, which used to be called Crispa tulips, have flowers that are fringed at the edges, giving them a soft, lacy look. They grow to about 2 feet. The colors are quite beautiful.

Lily-flowering tulips have a place in every garden. They are a fine contrast to the more formal Darwin, Darwin hybrid, and cottage varieties. Their elegant blooms have reflexing curved petals that stand majestically atop strong, tall stems for a bold but graceful statement. Colors are subdued but warm.

Multi-flowering tulips are a bunch-flowering variety that produce at least four full-sized flowers per stem, offering a very colorful display in a small area.

Parrot tulips. This flamboyant, exotic variety is a welcome addition to the May garden. Its blossoms are showy, fringed with scalloped plumage, and large flowers. They grow to about 20 inches.

Peony or double-late tulips are long-lasting, scented tulips that closely resemble peonies. Their large, fully double blooms are beautiful in both the garden and for cut-flower arrangements.

Rembrandt tulips are among the oldest of all tulips grown. You'll recognize them from paintings of the sixteenth, seventeenth and eighteenth centuries. They are known as 'broken tulips,' with each flower feathered and striped in different colors. Always a conversation piece in the garden.

Viridiflora or green tulips are delicately feathered with green on softly colored petals for an ethereal beauty all their own. These long-lasting tulips are appropriate in both bedding designs and as cut flowers.

Here is a list of the late-blooming tulips that tend to perennialize, drawn from the trial plantings of specific varieties of tulips for four years in conjunction with North Carolina State University. Similar results in your garden, no matter where it is, are most assuredly not guaranteed. For a reliable display, it is better to dig them up after bloom and discard them, and to plant new ones in the fall.

VARIETY	COLOR
Ad Rem	Red, edged yellow
Burgundy Lace	Red
Delmonte	White, fringed with purple
Don Quichotte	Red-orange
Duke of Wellington	White
Dyanito	Red
Gordon Cooper	Red-orange, edged red
Jimmy	Red-orange
Karel Dorman	Red, edged yellow
Kees Nelis	Red, edged yellow
Makeup	White, edged red

Here is a planting of a number of varieties of both Darwin and lily-flowering tulips, along with the tall, somber *Fritillaria persica*. Although many use tulips for formal effects, they can also be used in an informal garden.

53

The history of tulips is quite colorful, probably the most interesting of all plants. Prior to 1554, tulips had never been seen in Europe. That year, Austrian Emperor Ferdinand I sent a man named Ogier de Busbecque from Flanders, which at the time was subject to Austria, as his emissary to Constantinople, now Istanbul, in Turkey to negotiate peace with Sultan Suleiman the Magnificent. While traveling from Adrianople, he saw "an abundance of flowers everywhere—narcissus, hyacinth, and those that the Turks called 'tulipam,'" according to an account left by him. He bought some bulbs, "which cost me not a little," according to his account. Upon returning to Vienna, he planted them in the imperial gardens. They multiplied, word of their existence and beauty spread, and soon people all over Holland and Europe coveted the new prestigious flowers. This was the beginning of "tulip mania." In 1624, a red and white tulip with a base of a blue tinge sold at auctions for twelve hundred dollars. The next year the owner sold two propagated from the first for three thousand dollars. Shortly thereafter three bulbs commanded thirty thousand dollars. A few years later, the mania turned to madness, and the tulip market collapsed. A financial panic ensued, fortunes were lost, and some investors were driven to suicide. The government banned further tulip speculation, and the Dutch turned to hybridizing and growing bulbs commercially as they do today. By the end of the eighteenth century, tulips became a primary planting on the great estates of Europe and here in America. Both George Washington and Thomas Jefferson installed major plantings at Mount Vernon and Monticello.

In our garden we use the late-blooming tulips as an underplanting and a complement to the native American dogwoods (*Cornus florida*) and evergreen azaleas. When in bloom, dog-

woods are as spectacular as no other flowering tree. Through the years, we have tried many different varieties, but have found that the white *Cornus florida* 'Snowflake' and the rich, ruby red 'Cherokee Chief' have served us very well. In spring they offer a blizzard of glorious blooms, after which they leaf out with elegant, glossy leaves providing needed shade in various parts of the garden. In the fall, the foliage turns a deep mahogany red, and clusters of red berries emerge. The birds love them. In fact, every year the robins and the catbirds, before they make their annual pilgrimage to Palm Beach and other sunny places, devour them all. There have been times when we have had forty or fifty robins all eating their share at the same time. After the dogwoods lose their leaves, they serve as a sculptural backbone for the winter garden, with the snow-covered bark particularly beautiful.

To complement dogwoods, we plant the late-blooming tulips: Darwins, cottage, *Viridiflora* green, and lily-flowering. We use pink, pale yellow, white, rose, purple, lilac, and green. Remember that there is a time of bloom difference between Hybrid Darwins and Darwins. The Hybrid Darwins are finished blooming when the dogwoods and azaleas are just beginning, so they are the wrong selection if you want a spectacular display in tandem. Use the Darwins instead. Perennials, too numerous to list, also burst into bloom.

Unfortunately, about twenty years ago a disease surfaced that threatened to wipe out all of the dogwoods (*Cornus florida*) both in the wild and in gardens. Panic spread through the world of horticulture. There didn't seem to be anything that anyone could do to stop the progression and proliferation of the disease. It is called anthracnose and affected millions of the trees. Since that time, hybridizers have developed varieties that are resistant to the disease. Although the disease is still a threat and still affects some trees, it does not seem to be as virulent and destructive as it once was. Affected trees slowly die. Leaves brown, and branches become brittle and gray. This dying process takes about five years, but it is relentless. Spraying does not seem to help.

A friend of ours, who is almost always full of bad or depressing news, came to see the garden one spring. He pointed out that there were parts of our dogwoods that looked sick. He said we had better cut them down so they wouldn't spread the disease. One of our 'Snowflake' dogwoods is located in a very crucial spot in the garden, not only aesthetically but it also serves to shade the entire southern exposure of the house during the hot summer days. If we did lose the tree, it would take years for another to fill the void. Beyond that, the ashes of my basset hound, William, had been set beneath the tree when we planted it many years ago. We were quite depressed about it and then decided that we would not cut the tree down, but rather care for it and hope for the best.

The following two or three years, there was some more slow damage to the tree, but we persisted. It just didn't look as though it was dying, despite friends telling me to "cut it down and plant something else." That winter we had a rare ice storm here on the North Fork. One of our 'Cherokee Chief' dogwoods split right down the middle and had to be removed. But the 'Snowflake' had only been severely pruned by the splintering limbs. Next spring, there was a bounty of healthy, new growth sprouting from every branch. It almost seemed as though the tree was rejuvenating itself. It is now three years later, and it is more glorious than ever, looking, like everything else around here, including us, as though it has been here forever. It has, miraculously, rid itself of whatever affliction it had and is more vigorous and more beautiful with every passing year. Point being, sometimes you have to stick to your guns and, as with all that is alive, including human beings, have faith that in some way, nature will take care of things. And, by the way, *Cornus florida* self-seeds, so look for new seedlings beneath all of your dogwoods once they get to the berry-bearing stage. We have planted some in other parts of the garden and have given dozens of them away to friends. You have undoubtedly heard of the Kousa dogwoods. These dogwoods are not prone to anthracnose, have a white or washed-out pink color, and bloom somewhat later than the *Cornus florida*. They are included in the late-spring section of iris and peonies, since they bloom in tandem with them.

Along with the tulips and the dogwoods, the finishing touches are the evergreen azaleas, mostly in pink, rose, white, lavender, purple, or combinations thereof. There are so many different varieties available. Each year we add a few new ones to the late-spring scheme, usually waiting until the after-season sale when you can pick them up very cheaply. Some varieties have rosebud-shaped flowers, and there are frilled and ruffled versions and doubles. They grow from a dwarf 1 foot by 1 foot to 6 feet tall. But all are easily controlled by pruning judiciously when the plant is dormant in the

This shade garden is a recent addition. We found the outhouse abandoned near an old farm, moved it, and restored it. It became an instant focal point in the garden. It is also the place we go to listen to the sound of rain on the roof during summer showers.

Clockwise from top: We try to place bird feeders above beautiful plantings to attract colorful goldfinches and purple finches. We move them several times during the spring season to enhance the plantings. ■ Although it is an unlikely combination, these purple rhododendrons and orange-coral deciduous azaleas are a classic Paul Gauguin color combination, which is why we call this the Gauguin garden. ■ Think pink! Here, flamboyant pink tree peonies are interplanted among pink azaleas for a spectacular display.

winter. We buy them at nurseries, through mail-order sources, and even in supermarkets. We plant them as both specimens and in large sweeps, perhaps 10 to 15 feet long. Underneath our magnificent 150-year-old yew tree, a large 20-year-old planting of large-blossomed white azaleas serves as a backdrop for dwarf rhododendrons and camellias.

Be sure to include 'Robin Hill' azaleas in your scheme. The blossoms are enormous, from 3 to 5 inches across. They are very cold hardy, and the colors are stunning, soft pinks, rose pinks, pure white with yellow overtones, salmon red, and combinations thereof. They are dwarf and semidwarf, growing in mound-like habits. Our favorites are 'Hilda Niblett,' a soft pink with deeper rose overtones, and 'Olga Niblett,' pure white with yellow.

An entirely separate class of azaleas is the deciduous variety. These azaleas drop their foliage every fall. The enormous pom-pom-blossom clusters bloom on near bare wood. In what we call our woodland garden, we have mixed the evergreen azaleas with a kaleidoscope of deciduous azaleas. There is Girard's 'Hot Shot,' a brilliant brick red, almost orange evergreen, scores of pink and white, and pale lavender along with the deciduous, bright yellow Girard's yellow 'Pom Pom,' the brilliant orange Exbury 'Gibraltar,' deep scarlet 'Satan,' and scores of other pink, lavender, peach, white, and rose varieties. For whatever reason, within the azalea family colors that normally would clash in other parts of the garden all look absolutely stunning in this shady area of our garden.

Shortly after the azaleas are in full bloom, the standard-sized rhododendrons begin to present their spectacle with their extravagantly billowing clustered blooms. These are large plants, often growing to 12 feet, and must be judiciously pruned for small properties. In fact, in the Himalayas, Ireland, and Scotland, there are specimens that grow into 70- or 80-foot trees. Remember that most of the charming dwarf varieties of rhododendrons bloom long before the standard rhododendrons and have completed their bloom cycle before that of the standards begins. We are adding to the collection of dwarf rhododendrons every year. We have them in pink, white, scarlet, and deep purple, and last year we planted two 'Lemon Ice,' a beautiful pale yellow. The standard rhododendrons bridge the gap between the tulip-azalea-dogwood spectacle and the lilac, iris, and peony spectacles that follow.

Just a few words on the history of these fine plants. The *Rhododendron* group that botanically includes

Later in May, after the earlier pink and purple rhododendrons have bloomed, the shade garden is dominated by this bank of white azaleas. White spiraea blooms in the distance.

azaleas is one of the largest in the plant world. There are about 850 species, which grow all over the globe, and this doesn't include subspecies, hybridized varieties, or clones, which number near ten thousand. It was during the eighteenth and nineteenth centuries that British and other imperialistic powers of the era were exploring the world; and beyond imperialistic ambitions, scientists, naturalists, botanists, anthropologists, archaeologists, and zoologists traipsed through jungles and climbed mountains seeking all manner of undiscovered treasures. In 1656, the first rhododendron, discovered in the Alps, reached Britain. By 1900, three hundred different varieties were in cultivation. Today there are thousands.

Shortly after the tulips, dogwoods, and azalea are in full regalia, the laburnum arbor presents its annual glorious display that covers the entire side of the arbor. Laburnum grows naturally as a tree, and it is spectacular, growing to 30 feet and covered with lovely, wisteria-like yellow panicles. But if trained and pruned to an arbor, it is even more spectacular. Training laburnum to grow on an arbor is not an easy task. It takes years of tying branches over the structure to create an archway. Pruning is a semiannual chore that you must do to help shape the growing plants.

We first saw laburnum in full bloom at the late Rosemary Verey's Barnsley House. It was a "walk," rather than an arbor because it was about 50 feet long and covered with the hanging yellow panicles. She had planted hundreds of purple globe-shaped alliums beneath it. When we told our friend and artist-author-gardener Robert Dash about our "walk," he asked how long it was. I said 16 feet, to which he replied, "That is not a laburnum walk, it is a laburnum arbor."

Purple *Clematis* 'President' blooms at the same time as the laburnum, and we are still trying to find the right purple iris to plant beneath the arbor to complement the yellow panicles. Chives are used by some and are a sensible choice because they do bloom at the same time as the laburnum and are very easy to take care of. Just be sure, if you opt for them, that you cut off the seed heads after the flowers bloom, or you will have chives all over the place.

In the every-dog-has-his-day category: On the adjoining property, just behind our fence and arbor, there is a stand of pesky honey locust trees. They are very invasive, sending roots for scores of feet and then sending up shoots where you don't want them. The shoots are easily removed, but they can be a nuisance. However, once a year, in the spring, they sport white panicles of intoxicating, honey-scented blossoms. Lo and behold, they bloom at exactly the same time as the laburnum. Pure chance, but it does go to show that even one of nature's nastiest, most invasive plants does have something good to be said about it.

We do not have the space to grow the beautiful purple *Wisteria sinensis* (Chinese wisteria) as a vine because it grows very aggressively. And, there is a considerable amount of maintenance involved that we simply do not have time for. However, wisteria can be trained into a small tree form. We plan on adding that to the landscape next spring since it blooms in tandem with laburnum. And we intend to lengthen our arbor by another 16 feet, which will make it 32 feet long. I'm sure that the distinguished Mr. Dash will then concede that yes, it is now a "walk" and no longer an "arbor." Humph!

We are nearing the end of the spring season; however, with careful planning, there are still several more spectacles ready to delight us. The lilac season will soon be upon us, offering an intoxicating scent and lovely bloom to the garden. On a still spring day the air in the garden is heavy with the smell of lilac. It has been said that ladies who are particularly fond of lilacs tend to have a wandering eye during lilac season when it comes to affairs of the heart.

What could be more evocative of spring, of young love, of a bygone era than the intox-

The woodland garden has leafed out by the middle of May. The sweep of blue columbines has self-sown and becomes bigger and more beautiful every year.

icating scent of extravagant spring-blooming lilacs. Claude Monet grew and painted them at Giverny, Shakespeare wrote about them, Vincent van Gogh painted them, and Walt Whitman wrote "when lilacs last in the dooryard bloomed." In "The Wasteland," T. S. Eliot wrote, "April is the cruellest month, breeding Lilacs out of the dead land, mixing dull roots with spring rain." And Amy Lowell wrote in her poem "Lilacs":

Heart-leaves of lilac, all over New England,
Roots of lilac under all the soil of New England,
Lilac in me because I am New England.

Lilacs are ancient plants that have enchanted gardeners for centuries. Native to Russia and Poland, they were introduced to Western Europe during premedieval times. The oldest stand of lilacs in the New World is on Mackinac Island in Michigan, planted by French settlers in the mid-seventeenth century. They are tough plants that survive neglect, and are used by archaeologists as indicators of a settlement or domestic structure on a site because they have been planted for centuries in domestic gardens.

Just about the only planting that existed on our property when we bought the house was a stand of the common pale lilac-colored *Syringa vulgaris* on the north side of the house. It was quite ancient and somewhat overgrown, but the blossoms at the tops of the branches were at the level of the second-story bedroom windows. In late spring, when in bloom, the entire upstairs of the house is filled with their agreeable scent. You might want to think about growing lilacs if you have an appropriate area beneath your bedroom windows.

Although short, the lilac blooming season fills an important gap in the spring bloom sequence. In most parts of the country, lilacs bloom after the dogwoods, azaleas, and spring bulbs are finished. They bloom just before the early blooms of the peony, lupine, and bearded iris, so with a little planning in terms of location and variety, breathtaking displays of color are possible. And lilacs also attract colorful butterflies to the garden. When you select lilacs for your garden, don't stop at one. Buy as many as your budget and space will allow. You will never regret it.

There are scores of varieties of single and double lilacs available in white, cream, violet, blue, lilac, pink, magenta, and purple, blooming over a period of five weeks each spring. However, despite more than a century of hybridizing, the most popular lilacs are still

The purple and green ground-cover foliage sets off the lilac tree perfectly in this woodland garden. ■ At the end of May, bouquets of lilacs fill the house with their intoxicating scent. With a little preparation and conditioning, they will stay fresh for over a week. Without preparation, they will droop pathetically.

Syringa vulgaris, with their familiar single, pale purple blossoms, and the many hybrids bred from them: 'Sensation' (purple and white bicolored), and 'Krasavitsa Moskvy' (white with many layers of florets on each bloom), 'Ludwig Spaeth' (deep purple).

Easy to grow, lilacs are all midseason bloomers and grow to between 8 and 12 feet. During the nineteenth and early twentieth centuries, the Lemoine or French lilacs were hybridized, and more recently, the late Father John L. Fiala, a priest and hybridizer of lilacs, added many fine varieties to the list. Beyond *Syringa vulgaris*, other varieties merit attention. Korean pale lavender-pink 'Miss Kim' is a midseason bloomer, which grows to about 5 feet, has compact growth, and is immune to powdery mildew, making it an ideal choice for small properties. *Syringa reticulata* or Japanese tree lilac sports large creamy white blossoms in early summer and grows to from 20 to 30 feet with a spread of 15 to 20 feet. It is not suitable for small properties but is useful as a specimen tree. Early bloomers are *Syringa* x *hyacinthiflora*. These usually are in bloom with the dogwoods, azaleas, and tulips.

Here are basic instructions for planting a lilac: When you buy your plant, if it is container grown or B & B (balled and burlapped), water it and place it in a shady, wind-free spot until ready to plant. If bare root, soak it in a pail of water for at least 4 hours or overnight. If you are not ready to plant bare root stock immediately, after preliminary soaking, heel plants into the ground in a shady spot and keep well watered until ready to plant.

Select a site with at least 4 hours of full sun a day; however, the more sun the better, so if possible, select a site in full sun all day long. Lilacs prefer good drainage, so do not plant in a swampy area or where water remains for over a day after a downpour. Average garden soil is adequate. Since they are highly prone to powdery mildew, which does not hurt plants but looks unsightly, select a site with reasonable air circulation. If using lilacs as specimens, plant 10 to 15 feet apart. If using lilacs as a hedge, plant 6 feet apart.

As always, remember the old rule of thumb: A ten-dollar plant needs a twenty-dollar hole. So be sure to prepare the site properly. Dig a hole 2 feet across by 2 feet deep. If excavated soil is heavy in clay, mix in sand at the ratio of about one part sand to one part clay. Fortify with well-rotted compost or manure or sphagnum peat moss at the ratio of about one part additive to two parts excavated soil. If soil is very sandy, mix in well-rotted compost or manure or sphagnum peat moss at the rate of about one part additive to two parts excavated soil. In either case, mix in a good handful of 5-10-10 fertilizer.

Fill in the hole with fortified soil to the depth of about one foot. If container grown, remove lilac from container, loosen the root system, and set plant in hole at the level at which it grew in the container. If B & B, do not remove burlap cover. It will rot in the soil. Fold and cut away any fabric that juts out above the soil line. Set plant in soil at level at which it grew in the nursery. If bare root, cut off broken roots, spread them out, and set the plant at the level at which it grew in the nursery. Fill in hole with remaining fortified soil. Tamp soil firmly around plant ball or roots.

Water well and let water settle. After water has drained, fill in with additional soil and water once again. Keep plant well watered during its first year. If there has been no significant rainfall, water thoroughly once a week. If soil is waterlogged, wait until it has dried out some before watering again. Too much water can kill the plant. Place a wood chip mulch three feet around the plant. Do not use brick chips or stones for mulch because they retain heat and can damage the root system. Mulch conserves moisture, prevents weeds from growing, and eventually fortifies the soil when it breaks down.

If air circulation is poor or if summer is excessively wet, white powdery mildew may form on leaves. This is not harmful to the plant. If aesthetically objectionable, control by dusting the lilac with powdered sulfur. Rarely, if ever, will you have borer problems; however, once a season, check for borer holes in larger stems near the ground. If there is a severe problem, sawdust is usually present on the surrounding soil surface. Branches infested with borers should be cut off below the borer holes and burned or disposed of.

In late winter or early spring, remove dead and crisscrossing branches that rub together. As the plant matures, remember that stems from 6 to 8 feet tall and 1 to 2½ inches in diameter produce better quality bloom than taller stems of 4 inches in diameter or thicker. Remove these older, taller stems at the base of the plant. As soon as possible after bloom, remove or deadhead spent flower clusters. This directs the plant's energy into setting new flower buds for next year rather than into forming seeds. Do not prune lilacs after the Fourth of July, or you will remove forming flower heads. As always, to prevent spread of disease, sterilize pruning shears with a 10 percent solution of bleach and water before and after using.

If you have old existing lilacs in your garden and they need rejuvenating, try this three-year plan. The first year, immediately after bloom time, remove one third of the large growth at the base of the plant. The second year, remove another third, and the third year the final third. This forces vigorous, new, potentially blooming stalks to grow. If there is little or no bloom, the reason is probably that the plant is not getting enough direct sun and/or it must compete for nourishment and moisture with the roots of other nearby plants. Other possibilities are overfertilizing, poor drainage, pruning before bloom instead of after, and failure to deadhead spent blossoms after bloom time.

Some plants also in bloom during lilac season are Siberian and bearded (German) iris, peonies, lupines, poppies, a few very late tulips, bleeding hearts, and creeping ground phlox.

There is probably no bouquet of flowers more welcome than lilacs. The blossoms are extravagantly lush, and the scent is not overwhelming or sickeningly sweet but fresh, youthful, and invigorating. If you want early bouquets, you can force lilacs. When buds swell in spring, cut some branches and place in a vase of water. The buds will open within a week or two. If cutting lilacs in bloom, cut the flower stalks when they just begin to open. Be sure to condition the cut flowers as follows, or they will simply droop in a vase and die. Cut stems at a 45-degree angle. After you cut, pound woody stems with a hammer. Remove the bark and place the wounded stem in denatured alcohol for only three to five minutes. Precondition cuttings by placing in room temperature overnight. Be sure water covers three quarters of stem. Remove leaves below water level of vase. Before arranging, using a sharp knife, cut a slit 2 to 8 inches long up the length of the stem, depending on how long the stems are. The cut should be no more than one third the length of the stem. Place in room temperature water and change the water every two days. When you do, repound the stems with a hammer.

Here are some varieties which are readily available and recommended for easy growing:

VARIETY	COLOR
Annabel	Pink
Assessippi	Lilac
Blanche Sweet	Blue
Charm	Pink
Edith Cavell	White
Excel	Lilac
Katherine Havemeyer	Pink
Krasavitsa Moskvy	White
Ludwig Spaeth	Purple
Maiden's Blush	Pink
Ellen Wilmott	White
Miss Kim	Lavender-pink
Mt. Baker	White
Pocahontas	Violet
President Lincoln	Blue closest to true blue
Primrose	Pale yellow
Sensation	Bicolored, purple with white edges
Vestale	White
Victor Lemoine	Lilac

The following are the best selections for intense fragrance:

VARIETY	COLOR
Annabel	Pink
Assessippi	Lilac
Charles Joly	Magenta
Edith Cavell	White
Ellen Wilmott	White
Mme Lemoine	White
Paul Thirion	Magenta
Victor Lemoine	Lilac

The following minimum-chill lilacs thrive and are recommended for warmer climates such as Northern Florida and Southern California:

Lavender Lady
Blue Skies
Sylvan Beauty
Big Blue
Angel White

The following late-blooming lilacs, all *Syringa* x *prestoniae,* grow well and are recommended for the colder areas in Zones 2 and 3:

VARIETY	COLOR
Donald Wyman	Deep pink to red
James MacFarlane	Pink
Miss Canada	Pink

Although German or bearded iris, Siberian, and Japanese iris, along with lilacs and peonies, provide a spectacular end-of-spring display, here in our garden, we also grow dwarf, miniature, and median iris. The smaller iris offer earlier bloom and the medians are a reasonable substitute for the towering, tall bearded iris that are quite at the mercy of spring wind or rain. Staking the tall varieties is recommended if you have the time to do so. If not, opt for the medians, which usually do not require staking.

Bearded or German iris (*Iris* x *germanica*) are easily grown, long-lived perennials. Familiar to all, the flowers have three upright petals called standards and three hanging petals, called falls. A beard is in the middle of each fall. Their flowers come in every color of the rainbow. They flower in the spring (April to June depending on the cultivar), but some of the new cultivars reflower in the summer and fall. They are called rebloomers; however, they are temperamental and, depending on many factors, often do not rebloom. The second flower display is not as showy as the spring display but lasts into the fall. Here are the various classes:

Miniature dwarf (height 8 inches or less, 1-to-2-inch-diameter flowers). Early bloomers that are ideal for edgings, borders, or rock gardens.

Standard dwarf (height 8 to 15 inches). These bloom in midspring, and are slightly taller than the mini-dwarfs.

Intermediate (height 16 to 27 inches). Miniature tall (height 16 to 25 inches, small flowers), and border (height 16 to 27 inches). Most bloom just before the tall bearded iris and have the advantage of stronger, shorter stems that do not topple over in periods of heavy rain.

Tall (height 28 to 38 inches). These are the gorgeous queens of the iris world, with magnificent 6-inch blooms displayed on stems over 29 inches high. They bloom at spring's end, are available in every color of the spectrum, and include an incredible variety of color patterns and combinations.

Iris have been grown since ancient times. The name is derived from the ancient Greek name for the messenger of the goddess Hera, who was the queen of ancient Greece's heaven. As the fleur-de-lis, it was the symbol of the French monarchy for centuries. Today, it is traditionally used in decoration.

For best results, plant them in July, August, or September, not in spring or late fall, for newly planted rhizomes must be well established before the growing season ends. In areas with hot summers and mild winters, September or October planting may be preferred. Iris need at least a half day of sun. In extremely hot climates, some shade is beneficial, but in most climates they do best in full sun. They will survive in partial shade, but bloom will be diminished substantially. Well-drained soil is essential as rhizomes are prone to rot in wet soil. Plant on a slope or in raised beds if drainage is not good in the level parts of your garden. It is best not to water iris once they have been established unless there is a very long drought during the summer. If that is the case, be sure to water only the ground. Try to keep the foliage from getting wet, since this encourages disease. Good air circulation is also essential because it cuts down on potential disease and pest problems.

These median brown-toned iris work well in combination with the chartreuse leaves of the dwarf hosta planting in front of them.

Bearded iris need balanced, well-drained neutral soil. Raised beds will also help with drainage and are a *must* for areas with high rainfall. Add coarse sand to heavy clay to aid drainage. Work in a handful of superphosphate or bonemeal per square foot to a depth of about 10 to 12 inches. Never use any fertilizer high in nitrogen, since nitrogen encourages rot problems.

Because planting bearded iris must be done in a special way, we have included instructions here. To plant, dig a shallow dish-shaped hole in the ground. Form a mound in the center of the hole on which you set the rhizome. Then arrange the roots down along the sides of the mound and firm the soil around it. Cover the rhizome with soil until it is even with ground level. Try to use groups of three when you plant new iris. Place the fans of two divisions pointing to the outside rim of the hole and the other pointing to the inside. This helps to create a very natural look. Water well with a water-soluble fertilizer mixed to half strength. This helps settle the soil around the roots. A common mistake is to plant iris too deeply. Tall bearded iris clumps should be planted 12 to 24 inches apart, which gives the planting an immediate effect of maturity. *Never, never, never* mulch iris since mulch harbors pests and diseases that attack the rhizomes and the plants.

Because iris are so beautiful, it is worth the extra time and effort involved to deal with the few pest and disease problems that may occur. Leaf spot is one of them. After flowering, leaves may become dotted with small brown spots. Bacterial leaf spot has a watery, streaked appearance. Water-soaked margins around the spot turn yellow. Fungal leaf spots are rust-colored, drier, and more confined. Since disease organisms overwinter on old foliage, cut and destroy leaves of infected plants in the fall. Spray with a registered fungicide during extended periods of high humidity or rainy seasons. The most common of iris problems are iris borers. The first symptoms are small notches on the leaf edge or small accumulations of sawdust on the nearby ground in early spring. Iris later develop loose, rotted bases and holes in rhizomes. Bacterial soft rot readily attacks borer-infested plants. Carefully remove and destroy old leaves, stems, and plant debris in the fall. An insecticide can be applied to the rhizomes in the spring as new growth occurs.

When growing iris, perhaps the most important thing to remember is to be tidy and to always keep beds clean and free of weeds and debris, allowing the tops of the rhizomes to bask in the sun. Bloom stems should be cut off close to the ground after blooming. Healthy green leaves should be left undisturbed, but diseased or brown leaves should be removed. Plants that are growing well (good green foliage) may not need fertilizing. If you fertilize, apply ½ cup of 5-10-10 fertilizer per iris clump after flowering. Do not put fertilizer directly on rhizomes as it can burn them. Iris respond to shallow (1 to 2 inches) cultivation.

Keep your iris garden weed free. In early fall, cut leaves 6 to 8 inches from the ground, especially if foliage has leaf spot. When blooms are spent, snap them off at the base, taking care not to damage any new buds. After bloom season, cut stalks off close to the ground, being careful not to disturb rhizomes.

After a few years, iris will produce less and less bloom. That means that they are over-crowded and must be dug up, divided, and transplanted. Dig them up and cut away the old centers of the rhizomes. Use a sharp knife and continually sterilize it during the process by dipping it into a 10 percent bleach to 90 percent water solution. You do this to prevent the spread of bacteria. Rhizomes that are diseased will be mush and have a very acrid smell. Put them in paper bags and throw them in the garbage. Do not compost them. Once you have done this, cut all of the leaves at about 6 inches in a fan shape. To help prevent infection, soak the rhizomes for thirty minutes in a 10 percent solution of household bleach. Lay trimmed plants in a shady place for several hours so the cut ends can dry and heal. Replant only the healthy pieces about 8 inches apart in a sunny location with good drainage. It is a good idea to pick a new location so that any pests or diseases that lay in the soil will not infect the new plants. Plant as above. Be sure you are meticulous about watering these during hot, dry spells since they are just trying to get established. Established iris thrive on dry conditions.

Iris look best against a green shrub background. Scotch broom, mock orange, clipped privet, boxwood, snowball bush, and lilac all serve well as backdrops. Kousa dogwood is a spectacular companion planting with its blizzard of white blossoms. Plants that bloom in tandem with bearded iris are Siberian iris, peony, lilac, Asiatic lilies, lupines, liatris, Ori-ental poppy, columbine, early roses, and Shasta daisies. Good foreground plants are dwarf lavender, dian-thus, sweet alyssum, and rock cress. Once the iris have bloomed, you will want to fill in with color. Daylilies are the usual companions, but you must be careful to keep them in bounds, since they are more vigorous than iris. Annuals always help add color to an out-of-bloom spring spectacle.

What could be more glorious than a vase filled with a large bouquet of iris? The colors are stunning and the scent will fill a house. Cut iris when the first bud on a

In the beginning of June, the Kousa dogwood and the white 'Iceberg' climbing rose are a good combination. Notice that Mr. Chips, our cockapoo pup, home for the summer from boarding school, is right at home amid all the beauty.

stalk is nearly open. Add 1 teaspoon of sugar per quart of water to extend vase life. Remove spent blossoms each day. New buds will open daily.

Every year, the members of the American Iris Society (AIS) vote for their favorite hundred bearded iris. Both older and new cultivars are eligible. Here are the top ten for the year 2001. Most are readily available from mail-order sources and are generally easily grown, which accounts in part for their popularity.

VARIETY	COLOR
Dusky Challenger	Dark purple
Silverado	Light silver blue
Jesse's Song	White and violet
Beverly Sills	Pink
Conjuration	White and violet with white
Thornbird	Tan and violet with horns
Titan's Glory	Dark violet
Edith Wolford	Yellow and violet
Honky Tonk Blues	Hyacinth blue
Stepping Out	White and violet

When the sunlight shines through the Kousa dogwood blossoms, the effect is quite magical.

Along with bearded iris, the tough workhorse of the garden, Siberian iris bloom in late spring. They're rugged, easy to grow, pest and disease free, drought resistant, thrive on neglect, multiply readily, and adapt to all climates. They have tall, vertical, elegant foliage; gorgeous, delicate long-stem flowers for the garden and arrangements; and offer attractive seedpods for dried winter arrangements. What more could any gardener ask for? Siberians bloom from late spring to early summer, sometimes reblooming from midsummer to fall. They grow in clumps from 1 to 4 feet tall and 1 to 3 feet wide with an upright habit. Bloom colors are variations of white, blue, purple, yellow, and maroon.

We first discovered them early in our gardening experience. Initially, like most beginning gardeners, we wanted to have a beautiful rose garden. More than fifty hybrid tea and grandiflora roses grew here. Year in and year out, they had to be pruned, sprayed, and fertilized. We finally decided to phase out the rose garden, turning to plants that were less demanding on our time and energy. We still grow some roses, but only a very few old-fashioned and climbing varieties, which are practically disease and pest free and only require occasional pruning. The same held true for fruit trees. At one time we had fifteen different fruit trees. It was like having fifteen beagles, all of which required very separate attention and care. As with roses, pruning and spraying were major time-consuming tasks, and if we happened to be away and missed one of the crucial sprays, we ended up with a mess of inedible, ugly fruit that fell to the ground, attracting clouds of fruit flies. Beyond that, fallen fruit litters the property and can be dangerous for walking. But we do grow a fig tree. It is right against the house on a southern exposure and provides luscious figs for most of the coming summer

And so the search for easy, reliable plants began. Siberian iris were among the first to fill the bill. We now have about a dozen different varieties. Among my favorites are the white and pale yellow 'Butter and Sugar,' royal purple 'Caesar's Brother,' deep purple 'Nelson Blue,' violet and white 'Dance Ballerina Dance,' and medium blue 'Soft Winds.' And recently, there has been a very welcome development in the world of Siberian iris. There are now three new 7- to 12-inch-high dwarf Siberians available: medium blue 'Little Sister,' 'Little White,' and medium violet 'Annick.' They are the perfect size for our rock garden and add a touch of class in May and June.

If you order plants through mail-order sources, they will arrive with roots in a moist wrapping of some sort. Remove the wrapping and soak the plants in a bucket of water deep enough to cover the roots for twelve hours before planting. If you don't have time to plant them when they arrive, you can leave them in the water for up to a week. Change the water daily if possible. Siberians prefer full sun, but they will grow in semishade. They are not subject to mildew or pests. Ordinary soil is adequate; they do not like waterlogged soil. It is a good idea to improve the soil by working a substantial amount of sphagnum peat moss or compost into the planting hole at a ratio of about 1 part additive to 3 parts soil. Plant Siberians any time during the growing season with the tops of their rhizomes 1 to 2 inches below the soil surface. Water thoroughly and do not allow them to become dry until completely established. During the growing season, cultivate regularly to control weeds. A 1- to 3-inch mulch of straw, pine needles, or wood chips is helpful to retain moisture during prolonged dry periods, to keep the weeds down, and generally to dress up a flower bed. Do not mulch with peat moss or grass clippings as both pack down and become impervious to water.

As with bearded iris, if bloom becomes sparse, the reason is almost always that they need to be divided. With vigorous cultivars you may have to do this every third year. Less vigorous varieties are usually all right for five years. Dig the plants out of the ground in August or September. Cut them in pieces with a sharp knife. Replant as you would a new plant. Good companions that bloom around the same time as Siberian iris are pink, white, cherry red, and pale yellow herbaceous peonies, and perennial geraniums, particularly blue

Early June is the time when our Japanese iris (*Iris ensata*) bloom. They thrive in a boggy environment, so we have several varieties around our water garden.

'Brookside' and *Salvia* 'Blue Hill.' *Sedum* 'Brilliant' adds lovely succulent leaf texture, as does *Hosta fortunei* 'Marginato-alba.' Dwarf lady's mantle is excellent used in the foreground of a planting of iris. The fragile flowers of columbine and their equally delicate foliage contrast with the spear-like iris foliage. Annual pink 'Silene,' pink or white *Heuchera* (coral bells), Virginia bluebells, white bleeding heart, white- or pink-flowering astilbe, or salmon and pink Oriental poppies are all attractive companions to Siberian iris.

Some of the most popular varieties of Siberian iris are 'Lee's Blue,' which is a magnificent true blue; 'Super Ego,' another clear blue; 'Berlin Blue Moon,' vibrant blue; 'Caesar's Brother,' deep velvety purple; 'Orville Fay,' medium blue with darker veining; and the diminutive 'Little White,' which grows only to 12 inches.

The last of the major iris to bloom are the Japanese or *Iris ensata,* and what a dazzling display they offer. The enormous flat blooms atop 3- or 4-foot-high strong stems seem to float like giant butterflies over the plant. They range in bloom size from single blossoms to complicated 12-petal double blooms. Colors are white to blue-lavender, orchid-rose to deep violet or purple. Patterns of white veining over dark colors are particularly beautiful. Because they are easily grown from seed, there are a great many unnamed varieties extant. Many are equally as flamboyant and captivating as the named varieties.

Japanese iris need at least six hours of full sun a day; however, the more sun the better, so if possible, select a site in full sun all day long. Water is their most important requirement, so they thrive near water or where the planting area is only slightly above the water table. Plant Japanese iris in a spot with plenty of humus-rich soil for they are heavy feeders and require lots of organic matter for nutrients. They prefer acid soil. Japanese iris rhizomes must not be allowed to dry out before planting. Soak them in water for up to forty-eight hours before planting. Plant the rhizomes 2 to 3 inches deep in a shallow bowl-shaped depression and fill the depression with mulch. It will help catch and retain more water, Japanese iris's most important nutrient. Add a 2- to 3-inch organic or wood-chip mulch.

Another way to assure that Japanese iris get sufficient moisture is to dig out the planting area to a depth of about 16 inches. Line the bottom and sides with some heavy-duty rubber pond liner or other nonporous substance. Then mix peat moss with the soil at a ratio of about 2 parts peat moss to 1 part soil and water thoroughly. This will take some time and must be done slowly so that the water is absorbed into the peat moss rather than washed away. Once the soil is thoroughly wet, plant the iris. Keep well watered all during the growing season. After the first frost, remove and destroy old foliage. Destroying old foliage is helpful in controlling insects and diseases. Since Japanese are heavy feeders, scratch in a good handful of 5-10-5 fertilizer around each plant in early spring. Some popular varieties are:

VARIETY	COLOR
Asato Birako	Bright blue with white
Bellender Blue	Dark blue-violet
Enchanted Swan	White with hint of yellow
Haku-Botan	White
Nara	Dark purple
Oriental Fantasy	Ruffled white and mauve
Pink Pearl	Pale pink, darker in the middle
Shei Shonagon	Light blue
Waka Murasaki	Dark purple with white veins
Wine Ruffles	Dark red

The last of the great spring spectacles are the herbaceous peonies. Like all herbaceous perennials, they sport new growth in the spring, then bloom, and finally in the fall, the foliage turns brown and dies. Peonies come in every color except blue and green. There is every variation of white, pink, red, maroon, and yellow, often in interesting and wonderful combinations of color and form. They have single, semidouble, or double pompon flowers that bloom on lustrous, dark green foliage that remains attractive throughout the season. In some parts of the country they are called paeonies (pay-ee-oo-knees) and in others peonies (pee-oo-knees). Take your pick! It's like tomato-tomahto, potato-potahto, pecan-pecahn. And don't try to figure out which is correct English and which is incorrect. Discussions like that can only lead to nasty arguments and hurt feelings. Point is, they are regionalisms and as such are neither correct nor incorrect. The main thing is that we all understand what we are talking about.

Now here is an important word of advice: The flamboyant double pompon peonies are indeed a sight to behold; however, they must be grown in peony cages or staked. Once they have opened, even a gentle rain will cause the blossoms to bend to the ground, get splattered with mud, and look very sad. So we have learned that the answer is to stick to the single or the Japanese and anemone forms. These do not have heavy blooms and almost always remain in good shape after even a heavy rain. Peonies have different petal types from heavily ruffled to smooth, and some have rough, exotic-looking petal edges. Some have lovely fragrances. They thrive in enriched soil and in full sun. They grow from 24 to 48 inches, need plenty of moisture, and should be planted outdoors in August or early September.

Peonies were the original mainstays of the cut-flower business in the United States. They have been quite out of fashion as cut flowers for the past seventy years or so since gar-

Annual sweet alyssum self-seeds every year. Here it provides an attractive carpet for the deep pink tree peonies.

For years we grew the lavish pompon peonies but after every rain they ended up mud-splattered on the ground. The solution was to use only single, Japanese, and anemone varieties, such as this one.

deners and the cut-flower business concentrated on many of the more exotic annuals that were coming into popularity. Even amateur gardeners had ignored peonies for many years. However, recently peonies are gaining renewed interest for the same reason they were popular before; they are long-lived, often living more than fifty years and many times outliving the person who planted them. Some peonies have been known to live and flower as large shrubs for more than seventy years.

Originally from China, there are hundreds of cultivars that have been used medicinally and cultivated for over four thousand years. Nineteenth-century artists Manet, Renoir, Gauguin, and Delacroix all painted them. In China, poetry, paintings, and pictures on vases glorify the beauty of the peony.

Usually, peonies are long-lived undemanding garden plants that become more and more beautiful from year to year if they are left undisturbed. The final position for a peony should therefore be chosen very carefully since it doesn't like to be transplanted. As a rule, peonies flower in full splendor after three years. They need at least six hours of sun a day, with full sun preferred in northern areas and partial shade in southern climes. They prefer good drainage and average soil is satisfactory.

Plant in late summer or fall. Those planted in spring often are set back and sometimes die because they need time to get established. Planting peonies is somewhat like digging a foundation for a cathedral. First you dig a hole that is 15 inches deep and at least 30 inches in diameter. It is a lot of work, but once it's done it lasts for a hundred years or more. You never have to move the peonies or divide them if you choose not to, and they will continue to bloom. Make sure the soil you use to fill the hole is mixed with some sand and is loose and friable. Be sure that the root ends are facing downward and the crown (you can normally see the purple buds on it) is facing upward. Plant herbaceous peonies no more than 2 inches deep. It is important not to plant them too deep or they will bloom little or not at all. They like good drainage so do not pack the soil tight around the plant. Never place fresh manure or any organic matter that is not entirely composted near a peony since it can encourage rot or fungal problems. Keep the plant well watered during the first year.

In cold winter areas, it is a good idea to mulch peonies with tree boughs or clean straw after the foliage dies down. Clear away all dead and dying foliage in the fall because leaving it around the plant encourages pests and disease. Remove mulch as soon as the plant starts to grow in spring, or when the snow first melts off. During the growing season, place a wood-chip mulch to 3 feet from plant. Do not use brick chips or stones for mulch as they retain heat and can damage the root system. Mulch conserves moisture, prevents weeds from growing, and eventually fortifies the soil when it breaks down.

Peonies are almost always pest and disease free. But you should watch for *Botrytis paeoniae*. Here's how to tell if your peonies are infected with this blight. In warm humid weather the flower buds may be affected by fungus and turn black. This fungus wilts the young shoots in damp warm weather in spring. As a prevention, the plants may be sprayed with a fungicide. Wilting shoots must be cut back to the healthy wood and then sent out with garbage or burned. Check with your local nursery or garden center for chemical control. If bloom is sparse, the reasons are either lack of enough direct sunlight, competition for nourishment and moisture with the roots of other nearby plants, or that the crown of the plant was set in too deep. Again, 2 inches or less for herbaceous peonies is the rule. Good companions are alchemilla, campanulas, iris, lilacs, and many late-spring-blooming perennials.

The following list of early-, middle-, and late-blooming peonies, suggested by Kelhm's Song Sparrow, one of the country's largest peony growers, are all vigorous and easy to care for:

Another Japanese peony, not yet in full bloom, serves to set off the white star-shaped blooms of a Kousa dogwood.

EARLY	MIDSEASON	LATE
Barrington Belle Japanese, rose red	**Cheddar Charm** single, white, with gold center	**Betty Warner** Japanese, cranberry red
Burma Ruby single, bright red	**Cora Stubbs** Japanese, raspberry-pink	**Le Charm** single, cupped rose
Coral 'n Gold single, coral, with gold center	**Do Tell** Japanese, shell pink	
Aurora Sunrise Japanese, bright pink, with yellow center	**Doreen** Japanese, fuschia, with a yellow center	**Dawn Pink** single, bright pink
Eventide single, coral pink, cupped	**Miss Mary**	**Nellie Saylor** Japanese, wine red, with a cream-pink center
Ivory Atlas single, white-ivory	**Petite Elegance** single, magenta-pink brushed yellow	
Scarlet O'Hara single, deep red	**Rubyette** single, deep red	
	Fluffy single, white	

When exactly does spring end and summer begin? June 21 is the day on the calendar but because of very different climatic areas in North America, it is better to tag the date by the garden calendar. At what point in the sequence of garden spectacles does one season end and the other begin? All spring long, the bulbs, rock garden plants, azaleas and rhododendrons, spring shrubs, poppies, lilacs, iris, peonies, and so forth offer dazzling displays. By June 15, here on the East End of Long Island, all of these have bloomed with the last, the many varieties of iris, completing their annual spectacle. Iris begins blooming during the late winter, with the beguiling dwarf varieties the first to bloom in the rock garden. They are followed by the medians, the glorious tall bearded, then the Siberians, and finally the Japanese. Once they have finished blooming, the garden goes through a change. For several weeks there is sporadic bloom but nothing to speak of.

Out in our surrounding waters, the striped bass, perhaps the finest edible fish on this earth, and the small blue fish, called snappers, are running. And our summer raspberries are beginning to bear fruit. What a treat to be able to go out to the raspberry patch and pick a handful for morning cereal or for desserts. Because the birds are also addicted to them, we net the patch. When we do arrive to pick, there are always several catbirds darting about. They seem to be angry at us for taking our share of what is there. As more berries become

Summer in the Garden

available, we pick them and make our own raspberry vinegar. It is so simple! Just put a pint of ripe raspberries in a quart of white wine vinegar and let it sit out in the sun for about three weeks. When the raspberries have lost all of their color and the vinegar has turned a lovely red, it is ready to strain and use in summer seafood salads. Because of the time element, we do not grow many food plants, but we will never stop growing raspberries, salad greens, and tomatoes.

We have some friends who garden but refuse to grow tomatoes and, as far as I know, have never picked a sun-warmed tomato right off of the vine on a hot summer day. What a shame! I have even threatened to go over there some moonlit night, dig a hole in their perfect lawn, and plant several tomato plants. For centuries, every garden from the most humble to the grandest has always included food. What good is a garden that does not?

We always plant several of the 'Tom Thumb' dwarf tomatoes for our pet cockapoo, Mr. Chips. He loves tomatoes and can easily pick his own from the dwarf plants. When friends visit, he picks them one by one, runs with them, and places them before a guest. Needless to say, he has learned how to endear himself to people.

In early summer, the roses begin to bloom. Roses are summer flowers, but because of

Here, the deep burgundy foliaged *Cotinus coggygria* (smoke bush), which has feathery plumes in summer, is set off with a large planting of old-fashioned yellow yarrow. Yarrow is a good summer selection as it is drought resistant, pest and disease free, and blooms from late spring to fall.

'Heritage' is one of the new highly fragrant David Austin English roses that are a cross between hybrid tea roses and old-fashioned varieties, such as damask. The hybridization of English roses is the most important development in the rose world in more than seventy-five years. The contrast among the pale pink English rose 'Johann Strauss,' white *Digitalis* (foxglove), and the deep burgundy red *Berberis thunbergii* 'Crimson Pygmy' (barberry) is very effective. Barberry is one of the few plants that has deep red foliage during the spring and summer.

their demands on our time, alas, we have very few. Rose gardens peak in late June and again in September, blooming sporadically through the summer and into the fall. We have actually had roses in bloom at Christmastime. Among the few that we do have are a number of the sensational new David Austin English roses, which are a cross between hybrid teas and damask roses; climbers; some old-fashioned damasks; musk roses; and a Father Hugo yellow rose. All are almost pest and disease free. If there are two modern roses that we would plant in the garden, they are the creamy-pink, pale-yellow hybrid tea, 'Peace,' which is considered the finest rose of all time, and the *Grandiflora,* pink 'Queen Elizabeth,' which is considered the second finest rose of all time. Both are very pest and disease resistant, vigorous, and floriferous.

The early-blooming daylilies, followed by the midseason and late daylilies, will soon bloom. The hostas' foliage has leafed out and is at its best. If you have not yet planted annuals to fill in the color voids and spaces, it is time to do it. They will provide needed color throughout the rest of the growing season. Unfortunately, most annuals available in six-packs at nurseries and garden centers are clichés: dwarf marigolds, impatiens, ageratum, electric blue lobelia, scarlet salvia, and so forth. But at long last, more and more interesting varieties of plants are being offered these days. One of the best is *Calibrachoa,* or million bells. They look like mini-petunias and are available in cherry, pink, and yellow infused with pink, deep violet blue, and true pink. As they grow, they form mounds about 2½ feet across. There is also a whole world of blue salvia: *Salvia* 'Indigo Spires,' *Salvia* 'Purple Majesty,' *Salvia guaranitica.* Shop around, since many nurseries now offer some very interesting selections of annuals for the summer garden. You can also start your own from seed early in the spring, which often is the only way you can have some of the more unusual annuals in your garden. Because they are so easy to grow and so reliable, we do use shade-loving impatiens in our garden, but we stick to white or pink, rather than the more intense colors. They blend nicely with caladiums, which also love the shade.

Summer perennials like phlox, Oriental hybrid lilies, and the glorious white 'Casa Blanca' lilies start to bloom around the beginning of July. There is a difference between the blooms of these summer plants and those of spring. Summer blooms appear to be tougher, ready to wage battle against drought, heat, and torrential rainstorms. And they are more heavily scented than the spring flowers. We have found that summer flowers require less

intensive care and are more pest and disease resistant than spring flowers. Pink *Lycoris* is one of them. It is a lily that first sports foliage in early spring. The foliage browns and withers at the end of August, then stalks of flamboyant pink lilies bloom. Occasionally we throw a handful of bone meal on them and every year they get more and more beautiful, spreading in a very noninvasive and civilized manner.

The lush clusters of phlox—pure white, deep purple, orange-red, various pinks and lilac shades—last for weeks and weeks. They are vigorous, often have to be divided, can do very well without fertilizer, and sustain and bloom in drought, deluges, and dog-day temperatures. During the past decade or so, hybridizers have been successful in developing new varieties of phlox that resist the mildew that they are quite prone to. The mildew does not hurt the plant, but it does look unsightly. My friend and classmate Pierre Bennerup, the owner of Sunny Border Nurseries in Connecticut, one of the largest growers of perennials in the world, has come up with a homemade spray that will help control mildew. He says that 99 percent of the mildew derives from old leaves that have not been cleaned up from around the plants. Tidiness is the key to preventing mildew since spores may be in the air, but are much more likely to be in the soil. It is a good idea to mulch phlox with nonorganic materials, such as gravel. Do this in early spring. He recommends a spray made of ½ cup of baking soda, 1 gallon of water, and ½ teaspoon of cooking oil. Spray in spring, and then leave a small bottle of the liquid near the phlox and spray it whenever you walk by. Non–mildew-resistant varieties should not sport mildew if you do this. Some varieties

In the heat of summer, bright contrasts seem to work well. These brilliant fuschia cosmos combine well with the tiny yellow mini-zinnias below. ■ Combining summer-blooming perennials with annuals is always a good idea. In the background are perennial lemon lilies and white phlox 'David.' Annual cleome, ageratum, red zinnias, sweet alyssum, and pink verbena complete the picture. ■ Many water lilies (*Nymphaea* spp.) are hardy in the North. This lovely 'Pink Sensation' remains open in the afternoon.

that he recommends are *Phlox paniculata* 'David,' 'Blue Paradise,' 'Eco Pastel Dream,' 'Eco Purple Spotlight,' 'Robert Poore,' and 'Speed Limit 45.' "Two older varieties that have always been mildew-resistant for me are 'Eva Cullam' and 'Sir John Falstaff,'" said Bennerup.

Summer is the time to relax and enjoy the garden. The spring planting of perennials, shrubs, and trees is over, and summer planting is not recommended. Except for minor maintenance and deadheading, the garden offers peace, beauty, a wondrous world of plants, and a perfect place for entertaining friends. The evenings get longer and longer.

There are also many water plants in our pond. Lovely yellow water lilies nod their tousled blond heads in the sun. Elegant pink lotus, with its gently gyrating, enormous jade green leaves, resembles a flower-bedecked geisha cooling herself with a large fan. Bulbous water hyacinth majestically floats across the water like an armada in full sail. We also have delicate-leafed papyrus, water lettuce, and parrot feather.

We like to use plants that are heavily scented in that part of the garden. These include lemon verbena, chamomile, lavender, acidanthera, Corsican mint, heliotrope, sweet alyssum, and a collection of old-fashioned scented geraniums—lemon, rose, lime, and pine—which add rich foliage texture. We place them close to the sitting area so that when we entertain, we can encourage our guests to snip off a leaf here and there and enjoy the natural aromas offered. The scents are at their best in the evenings, not under the glare of the hot summer sun. And our dwarf *Magnolia grandiflora* 'Little Gem' sports its enormous blossoms, and the scent floats down through the garden.

As the years pass, we find that we always entertain our friends pondside. And during the hot tropical nights of late July and August, we spend many long evenings there. So we began to light the water garden at night. But we did not use electric lights, except to light the distant trees. We use only natural light, votive candles with Indonesian lanterns, French mini-hurricane lamps, Mexican tin lanterns, Chinese paper lanterns, Japanese stone lanterns, and Danish frosted light holders. We light the lamps and lanterns after dusk, and they highlight the iridescence of the white flowers. Like the Boulevard de la Croisette in Cannes or an aristocratic lady of gentle birth, our garden wears its diamonds only after dark.

At sundown in June and on into July, the fluorescent blips of light from the fireflies are hypnotic as you try to follow one of them just by watching a trail of twinkling lights. A flood of memories is released, and you relive the endless summers of childhood. To keep mosquitoes away, we use only citronella lamps and old-fashioned punks. The gentle melodic gurgling of the cataracts in our water garden is soothing, almost tranquilizing. Moths are the ballerinas of the dark, never seen in daylight. At night, they frolic near the candles and lanterns, creating a dance of the moths right before the eyes. We have created a world of sheer magic in our water garden at night.

Our water garden starts as a spring garden for it is then that we put it in order and flick the switch that starts the enchantment for yet another season. But in the summer, like the rest of the garden, it dons its summer "whites" and prepares to properly host such events as

There are many varieties of hardy yellow water lilies available. This one, 'Texas Dawn,' is one of the hardiest. ■ This pink, native American lotus (*Nelumbo lutea*) is hardy, but when cold weather sets in, you must sink it down into the deepest part of your water garden. Four feet is recommended. After the petals fall, pods can be picked and used in dried flower arrangements.

Koi and goldfish splash about in our pond in the summer. Try hand-feeding them. They nibble very gently. ■ White *Iris ensata* (Japanese iris) also shimmers in the evening light by the pond. This is the last in the series of iris spectacles, usually blooming in the beginning of June.

alfresco dinners, garden parties, the annual birthday extravaganza (at this gathering we ask that all of the ladies wear long white dresses and flowered hats, and that the men wear white ducks), croquet tournaments, badminton matches, conga lines, Charleston contests, serious drinking, and other diversions of a gentler time.

In this case the summer "whites" are sensuously scented flowers that take on a sparkling luminescence in the twilight and then again in the moonlight. Pure white *Lilium orientalis* 'Casa Blanca' (Oriental lilies), white *Hibiscus* 'Diana,' white *Phlox* 'David,' and other white perennials and annuals all are abloom. In the evening, the climbing moonflowers open, along with *Datura* (angel's trumpets). Datura sports great numbers of enormous pure white trumpet-shaped blooms that also offer a heavenly scent. They all open together sometime between 6:00 and 7:00 P.M. You can literally sit and watch them unfold, almost like a choir of angels singing to the heavens. This spectacle takes place every evening and lasts about fifteen minutes. And it is during the summer that our lovely pink and white lotus in the pond offer their flamboyant spectacle. As dusk and then darkness descends, we light the lanterns, lamps, and candles, break out the Canada Dry, turn on the music, and as F. Scott Fitzgerald wrote in *The Great Gatsby,* "the party has begun." And here, it doesn't stop until chilly autumn weather sets in.

Whenever there is a full moon, we take time to lie down on the grass and gaze at the heavens. We turn off the outdoor night-lights and enjoy the garden in the moonlight. There are events in the heavens all year round, but every August there is a spectacle few people ever take the time to enjoy, the meteor showers of the seven sisters, the Pleiades. There are usually reminders about it on the nightly weather reports and in the newspapers.

You should provide a sheltered spot in the garden where you can sit and enjoy summer showers. There is nothing quite as refreshing as sitting under a shelter with the sound of raindrops on the roof and the cooling breezes that accompany the showers. Thunderstorms are almost always welcome during the summer since they usually signify a change in the weather; a cold front passing through is always a treat. We sit on our porch and watch the thunder and lightning and literally feel the temperature drop ten, fifteen, or even twenty

Counterclockwise from top: We have chosen white 'Casa Blanca' lilies as part of the setting for our lower pond. Their heady scent adds a very sexy touch to the garden when evening is nigh. And their white petals shimmer in the evening light. ■ This elegant candelabrum with votive candles in it adds lovely light to the planting of white *Datura* (angel's trumpets), which open in the evening. ■ As dusk settles in the evening, we light these tiny yellow lanterns, which come from Indonesia. The effect is peaceful and, as you can see, breathtaking.

82

Clockwise from top left: Here is our outdoor living area, right next to the water garden. It is where we spend all of our leisure time during the summer. Annual purple heliotrope in the rock garden and other highly scented flowers fill the air with intoxicating perfume. ■ This view of the upper pond, taken from above, shows hardy 'Pink Sensation' water lilies in full bloom, as well as the plantings on the banks of the pond. ■ Mandevilla and moonflowers climb up the porch trellis, and there are quite a few containers planted with rose- and lemon-scented geraniums and lemon verbena, and pots of parsley, chives, and celery for quick fixes for salads. ■ One year, we grew tropical water lilies in the upper pond. These are a brilliant blue and combine well with the 'Texas Dawn' yellow lilies in the lower pond and the callas to the side. In the fall, remove them from the pond and dispose of them. Wintering them indoors is, unfortunately, a complicated process. ■ Here the yellow light of the lantern combines well with the yellow calla lily blossom. We like calla lilies and grow them every year around the pond. Most gardeners know of them, but very few grow them.

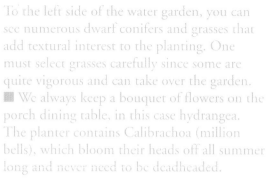

degrees by the time the storm has passed through. We have designed a porch landscape since we often eat dinner by candlelight there. Moonflowers, morning glories, and tropical mandevilla grace the trellises, and a dozen large terra-cotta pots contain herbs, aromatic annuals, and scented geraniums.

And yes, there is a ghost in the garden. I know who she is, and the times of her visits are quite without logic. Sometimes she appears in the afternoon, sometimes at night. And

I know that she is happy. Years before her death she said, "Someday I'll have a beautiful garden like this and find peace." I hope she has. But that is a story for another time.

Another summer pastime we look forward to is the collecting of wild mushrooms, and they grow all over the place out here on the East End. The first to make their appearance are the puffballs. If you pick them while they are still quite firm, they make an excellent soup. Brilliant orange and bright yellow peppery chanterelles, so prized in France, are there for the taking as are the wonderful boletus, known as cepes or porcini. The tiny angel's trumpets resemble small black trumpets and taste very much like truffles. The chicken-of-the-woods, an enormous sulfurous yellow mushroom that grows at the bottom of trees, is one of our favorites. You must pick them, cut away the tough parts, and then blanch them. Then you bread them and gently sauté them. You know you are eating something special, but are not sure if it is very tender chicken or very tender veal.

We used to have a mycology club out here, but those who knew all about that sort of thing, all middle Europeans, have long since passed on. Wild mushrooms almost always grow in areas under oak and pine trees and usually appear after a rain. However, don't pick and eat them unless you know or are with someone who does know which ones are edible and which ones are not. There is only one that will kill you, the deadly amanita, but there are plenty that will make you quite sick. I remember one time years ago when a colleague offered to take me to the oyster beds where the wild oyster mushrooms grew. They were there for the taking. But he made me promise not to show anybody else where they were.

The mixture of caladium in this planter dress up the shade area of the porch. We find them far more interesting to use than impatiens. They are grown only for their colorful foliage.

He said, "If you do, I'll have every Greek in Astoria out in your mushroom patches." He is a Greek Cypriot and grew up in the part of New York that is primarily Greek.

I don't care where you live, or how much time you or others spend tending it, no garden is at its best in August. The summer drought and high temperatures wreak havoc on plantings. The spectacles offered by glorious spring-blooming shrubs, trees, and bulbs have placed their mantles of lovely color in mothballs until next spring.

But there are a number of plants that will provide sequential spectacles in your summer garden. *Hemerocallis* (daylilies) are perhaps one of the toughest and most reliable of all perennials. There are early, midseason, and late varieties, which range in height from the dwarf 8-inch plants to more than 3 feet. You cannot have enough of these in your garden. Flowers bloom for only one day, then the following day another follows on the same stalk. Each plant flowers from three to six weeks. The color range is vast and more and more new varieties are available each year. There are single and double blossoms. Foliage is a medium green that remains attractive in the garden until a killing frost. And if you cook Chinese food, the buds of the flowers are the same lily buds used in that cuisine. The second indestructible perennial is hosta. Grown primarily for their foliage, you can fill all shady areas with them. There are dwarf, medium, large, giant, and super-giant varieties. They sport leaves in green, blue, yellow, white, and combinations thereof. They are a godsend to the busy gardener. As with daylilies, you cannot have enough hosta in your garden. Both plants grow vigorously and can be divided every third year to make more.

Most gardeners do not think of summer-blooming bulbs, but they fill a gap between early summer bloom and the fall-blooming perennials and the fall colors of shrub and tree foliage. In our garden we always have substantial plantings of some of these, primarily lilies. Here is a chart of the sequence of bloom of the summer bulbs that we use in the garden. In all zones, these bulbs are planted after all danger of frost is gone. There is slight variation in blooming dates, but generally, because of the warm summer weather, bloom time is the same in much of the country.

In our shady woodland garden, we always dress it up with brilliantly colored tuberous begonias and caladium.

VARIETY	BLOOM TIME
Caladium	Early summer to fall
Tuberous begonia	Early summer to fall
Colocasia (elephant's ear)	Early summer to fall
Lily, Asiatic hybrid	Early summer
Lily, Tiger	Midsummer
Lily, Aurelian hybrid	Mid- to late summer
Lily, Oriental hybrid	Mid- to late summer
Crocosmia (Montbretia)	Mid- to late summer
Zantedeschia (calla lily)	Mid- to late summer
Acidanthera (Abyssinian gladiola)	Midsummer to fall
Gladiola	Midsummer to fall
Dahlia	Midsummer to fall
Lycoris	Late summer

The summer blooming bulb *Acidanthera* (Abyssinian gladiola) has a lovely aroma and combines well with the purple verbena.

There are other summer bulbs, and we have grown almost all of them, but because they require special care, we do not recommend them. Keep in mind that this is a very personal opinion, based on experience. For example, *Agapanthus* is a sensational plant, but it requires special indoor care over the winter, which we do not have time for. *Anemone* and *Ranunculus* grow well and winter over for us here in Zone 7A, but this is as far north as they will survive winters. Gloriosa lily, *Hymenocallis, Sparaxis, Ornithogalum, Zephyranthes,* and *Tigridia* all offer lovely bloom for the specialist, but they require special growing conditions and care. The scent of tuberose is just too heavy for our summer garden, and canna lilies are too garish for us. Some of the newer dwarf varieties are somewhat more subtle.

Except for *Crocosmia,* lilies and *Lycoris,* which you treat as hardy perennials, the following bulbs are tender in most parts of the country and must be planted in late spring, after all danger of frost is past. Since they are tender, you must dig them in the fall and winter them over. Dry, clean, and then store them over the winter in dry peat moss or vermiculite in a cool, dry, dark place. Then replant in the spring.

Acidanthera (Abyssinian gladioli, peacock orchid) Creamy white with mahogany centers and 2-inch star-shaped blossoms on 18- to 24-inch spear-like, medium green foliage. Plant in full sun or partial shade, in ordinary soil, in late spring after all danger of frost is over or early summer, 3 inches deep and 4 inches apart. If heavy rains are common in your area during the summer, stake plants when 1 foot high. Water during summer drought. If you are north of Zone 7, treat as annuals and buy very inexpensive new corms each year. The blossoms exude a heavy, provocative perfume, more pronounced during the torpid heat of midsummer evenings.

Crocosmia (Montbretia) These are very reliable and very spectacular. Bright red 'Lucifer' is the best, but there are also yellow and orange varieties. Blooms are 1½ inches on 24- to 48-inch stalks with spear-like, medium green foliage. At one of our garden tours several years ago, we potted up about twenty of these and sold every one of them. Plant in full sun, in ordinary soil, in late spring, after all danger of frost is past, 3 inches deep, 4 inches apart. Scratch a light dusting of 5-10-5 fertilizer into soil when plants emerge and again three or four weeks later. Stake plants when 1 foot high. North of Zone 7, order and plant new corms each spring.

Dahlia There are hundreds of varieties of these old-fashioned, reliable plants, with blooms ranging in size from tiny, button-like flowers to those as big as dinner plates. They are all easy to grow, and with proper planning, you will have a mid- to late-summer spectacle. Plant the roots in late spring, after all danger of frost is past, in full sun or light shade, in well-drained soil fortified with sphagnum peat moss and well-rotted compost. Water throughout the season and mulch with a 2-inch cover of wood chips or rotted compost to conserve moisture. There were a few years when the dahlias that were left in the ground made a comeback the following year; however, they usually don't. Rather than going through the task of digging up, drying, and storing the bulbs, throw them out and buy new ones each year. They are very reasonable, and it is not worth the effort to try to save them.

Gladiola Most gardeners loathe gladiolas. They associate them with floral funeral pieces and so do not plant them. Too bad they have such a reputation because they can be used to great advantage in the summer garden. They are rather stiff when they bloom, but we have used them successfully in informal plantings. Do not plant them in rows with string support on either side, but plant them in clumps and then let them flop over to a certain extent, providing support with string tied to low support canes or peony cages. The effect is loose and informal. Blossoms come in every color of the rainbow on 1- to 5-foot stalks with medium green, spear-like foliage. Plant in full sun, in sandy soil, in late spring after all danger of frost is past, or early summer for later bloom, 6 inches deep, 5 inches apart. Since we live in Zone 7A, our gladiolas winter over in the ground. If you live farther north, treat them as annuals and buy and replant new ones each year.

Lilium (lily) With a large planting of lilies, a summer spectacle is assured, in June with Asiatic lilies, July with Oriental lilies (*L. speciosum*) and tiger lilies, and in August with Aurelian hybrids. There are lesser varieties as well, but these three are the most commonly

Our perennial garden, which has a very natural and somewhat wild look to it, peaks in summer. Bright red *Crocosmia* 'Lucifer,' which attracts hummingbirds, a number of varieties of veronica, astilbe, and daylilies all add colorful touches. ■ Pink lilies, red climbing rose 'Blaze,' and blue pansies all welcome visitors to the gazebo in a nearby garden. ■ Pink Asiatic lilies and deep burgundy *Heuchera* (coral bells) combine well in this summer planting.

Oriental lilies are a great favorite of many summer gardeners, and here they set off the white-barked river birch trees nicely. Pink Asiatic lilies and dwarf white Shasta daisies are a nice combination in this summer planting.

used in gardens. They come in all colors except blue. Depending on the variety, lilies may have 4- to 8-inch star- or trumpet-shaped blossoms on 2- to 7-foot stalks with glassy, dark green leaves. Plant in full sun or partial shade in enriched soil. Set bulbs 6 to 8 inches deep, with small lily bulbs 6 inches apart and larger bulbs (those the size of a fist) 18 inches apart. Stake taller varieties' stalks as they grow, but be careful not to drive the stake too close to the stalk because you might injure the bulb. Shorter varieties, such as hybrid Asiatic lilies, usually do not need staking. Lilies are among the few hardy summer-flowering bulbs, and they do not have to be dug up in fall and stored indoors over the winter. Use them in perennial borders and island beds for masses of color among shrub borders, or incorporate them in foundation plantings. A bonus of planting lilies is that they attract hummingbirds. These are the varieties we recommend:

Aurelian hybrids (trumpet lilies) These are the towering trumpet lilies that can grow to 8 feet. They look magnificent as a backdrop for a very wide border, but for most plantings they are too tall. We used to grow them but ran out of telephone poles to support them.

Asiatic hybrids These are the earliest blooming of the lilies, are very reliable, and increase in beauty each year, as long as you protect them from rabbits when they first poke up through the ground in late spring. They grow to between 2 feet and 4 feet, depending on the variety, and rarely require staking. The flower spike is compact with many blooms, some in solid colors, others speckled. Be very careful when selecting colors, as some can be quite startling, even garish.

Oriental lilies (*L. speciosum*) Many consider Oriental lilies the most beautiful of all. They bloom in midsummer. Colors are pink, rose, white, or gold and combinations thereof. Although they can grow to 5 feet, they rarely need staking. And there are dwarf varieties available that grow to only 2 to 3 feet. Their scent is heavy, particularly during summer evenings.

Tiger lilies (*L. lancifolium*) Most of these varieties are spotted, with the petals turned back. Each produces from twelve to twenty flowers per stem. They reach a height of 3 to 4 feet and bloom in midsummer. Here again, be careful in your color selection, as some varieties tend to be garish.

***Zantedeschia* (calla lily)** Dwarf callas have become very popular plants in the past decade, and thanks to hybridizers are now available in a large selection of colors. We treat them as annuals and replant every year. Flowers are about 3 inches high on 1-foot stalks in cream, yellow, pink, lavender, purple, crimson, orange, and bright red over heart-shaped leaves. Plant in full sun, in soil fortified with peat moss, 2 inches apart and 4 inches deep, after all danger of frost is past. Maintain even moisture until blooming ends. We like the dwarfs; however, our favorite is the giant yellow *Z. elliottiana,* which never fails to provide a lavish display on the banks of our water garden. They are not hardy and we do not try to winter them over because the one year we did, they rotted. We purchase new ones every spring. The classic white calla, *Z. aethiopica,* is the most spectacular of all, but requires a considerable amount of expertise to grow in the average garden. They thrive only in boggy conditions, or in water. We haven't gotten around to it yet, but one of these years we will try our luck.

The hanging varieties of tuberous begonias are particularly effective in window boxes. Our long-haired domestic cat, Droushka, spends the entire summer sitting in this window.

Lycoris squamigera (spider lily) This is one of those plants that surprises us every year. In the spring, broad strap-like foliage grows, thrives, and then by June browns and dies. At that point, we always forget about them. And then, in late summer, stalks much like those of amaryllis shoot up from the bulbs sporting lovely pink lily-like blossoms. *L. squamigera* is the only variety that is hardy throughout most of the country. They multiply freely and after a few years present quite a spectacle in August. Plant in early summer with top of bulb just beneath soil surface. Ordinary soil, full sun or partial shade, and watering during summer drought when they are in bloom is all they require.

Tuberous begonia, caladium, and *Colocasia* (page 22)

Most of us think of spring as the season for glorious floral displays of shrubs and flowering trees to complement the spring bulb plantings. Dogwoods, azaleas, *Rhododendron, Spiraea, Magnolia soulangiana,* flowering cherry, peach, and plum all make their statements. However, there comes a time in every gardener's experience when you begin to realize that there are indeed shrubs and flowering trees for summer, foliage for fall, and even shrubs that provide interest in winter by showing off colored bark and brilliant berries. But what about those August dog days? Take heart for there are shrubs and trees that bloom during the hot summer and subsequent cooler fall months. We started planting summer-blooming shrubs about ten years ago, and some of them are now reasonably mature and provide a lovely backdrop of bloom for the summer bulbs, annuals, and perennials.

Here are some varieties that we have used effectively and are just waiting to dress up your garden. Most of them will thrive in Zones 6 to 9, with many growing well in protected areas of Zone 5. However, *Vitex* (Chaste tree), crape myrtle, and *Hydrangea macrophylla* need a warmer climate and are reliably hardy only in Zone 7 and those farther south. However, as always, nothing ventured nothing gained. They may thrive farther north if installed in a sheltered area of your garden. Although the summer shrubs included below tolerate partial shade, most grow more vigorously if planted in full sun, with the exception of *Hydrangea* 'Variegata' (variegated lace-cap hydrangea), which prefers shade. Other beautiful blooming shrubs also decorate the summer landscape. Some are:

Abelia chinensis (Chinese abelia) For a lovely display from July through September, these highly fragrant, white and reddish-pink blossoms fit the bill. These plants are vigorous growers, reaching 5 to 7 feet high and 7 to 8 feet wide when fully grown. Tough and reliable, with handsome dark green foliage that is semievergreen in the north and evergreen in the south, they like full sun. Pest and disease free and drought tolerant when established, they are among the most attractive of all blooms to butterflies. Abelia adapts to many kinds of soils as long as it is well drained. Prune lightly after bloom period to maintain shape and keep within bounds.

Buddleia davidii (butterfly bush or summer lilac) These are showy summer-blooming shrubs that bear beautiful fragrant spikes of flowers on long stems. Each spring, cut entire plant down to about 6 inches high, since flowers bloom only on this year's growth. The shrub grows rapidly each year, from 6 to 8 feet high and 4 to 6 feet wide, and is not fussy about soil. The foliage is deciduous. Leaves are long and narrow, colored dark green with a silvery white underside. If you deadhead spent blooms, shrub will continue to bloom until, and well after, frost. Occasionally, they will self-seed. *Buddleia* is especially attractive to butterflies. Tiger swallowtails, monarchs, mourning cloaks, and even hummingbirds swarm to the blossoms all during the season.

White and magenta phlox and deep pink *Althea* (hibiscus) are tough plants that require minimal care during the summer. Be sure to deadhead both at the end of the season for they tend to self-seed prolifically.

We prefer either the white or the more vibrant colored bloomers, as the paler colors tend to fade in the light of the intense hot summer. Some varieties we like are 'Black Night' with intense, very dark, violet-purple flower spikes; 'Pink Delight' with large dense conical clusters of bright pink; 'White Bouquet' with stunning snow-white blossoms; 'White Profusion' with pure bright white flower spikes; 'Maine Purple' with reddish purple flowers. They do self-seed, but usually are not true to color, reverting to the common pale purple. We have found that the flowers of the yellow and white varieties do not hold their color well, and the blossoms brown shortly after they open. Keep butterfly bushes clipped in order to attract butterflies. See page 94 for more information on attracting butterflies to your summer garden.

Caryopteris x *clandonensis* (hybrid bluebeard) Not generally known, these wonderful plants offer rare blue blossoms from midsummer to fall. They are charming small shrubs that sport clusters of small, medium to dark blue flowers. Foliage is dark green or greenish gray, with small leaves, providing a pleasant background for the blue blossoms. This easy-to-grow plant grows in a mound shape, about 2 feet high by 2 feet wide. And it often self-seeds, providing you with more plants. Before planting, fortify soil with rotted manure or compost or a handful of 5-10-5 fertilizer, as *Caryopteris* prefers rich soil.

It is best to select some companion plantings, because the subtle shades of *Caryopteris* can be lost in a shrub or perennial border. Combine it with pink 'Fairy' rose and silver-colored betony or dusty miller. In the spring, cut back the entire plant from 2 to 4 inches above the ground since plants bloom on the year's new growth. Although the scent is not sweet, it is pleasantly herbal and reminiscent of verbena. One of the best varieties available is 'Blue Mist' with deciduous, silvery gray foliage setting off a lavish display of powder-blue flowers. It blooms from midsummer to fall, with a compact branching habit. Another favorite is 'Dark Knight' with deciduous, darker green foliage than 'Blue Mist,' deep purple-blue flowers, and grows 2 feet high by 2 feet wide.

Clethra alnifolia (summersweet) Try to find a dwarf variety of this since the standard variety grows from 9 to 15 feet. The pretty pale pink or white feathery blossoms bloom in late July and early August, with the foliage turning a brilliant yellow-orange in the fall. The scent, as with most summer-blooming shrubs and trees, is quite attractive, and will perfume the air around it during the long summer evenings.

Franklinia (Franklin tree) No summer garden should be without this prize. Originally discovered in Georgia by John Tradescant, the British botanist, and named after Benjamin Franklin. By 1790, there were no more of these trees left growing in the wild. The fragrant, large, single, white flowers, which resemble camellia blossoms, are as much as 3 inches in diameter and have a center mass of yellow stamens. *Franklinia* starts blooming in August and blooms right on through until there is a killing frost. The deciduous foliage in autumn is a gorgeous rich orange and red. In the South it can be grown as a tree, but in Zone 5 it is best to grow it as a shrub with many branches coming from the ground. A severe winter will kill the above-ground branches but the roots remain alive and send up new shoots the following year.

Hibiscus syriacus (rose of Sharon or althaea) These old-fashioned plants have been gentrified. *Et comment!* The common rose of Sharon has small hibiscus-like blossoms in ugly magenta or white with red centers, and self-seeds everywhere, to the point they are generally considered junk trees. Prior to acquiring some of the new hybrids, we spent years pulling out errant seedlings. Now we are trying very hard to kill those that are left. We have chopped them down, and each year they send up new shoots. And five years later, I'm still pulling up errant seedlings. Like Rasputin, they just won't die!

Butterflies find the pollen in *Buddleia* (butterfly bush) irresistible and will flock to a planting from early through late summer. This is a tiger swallowtail. Monarchs, sulfurs, mourning cloaks, and many fritillaries and black swallowtails all visit the planting.

The improved selections are sterile triploids that have a longer blooming season and thicker textured petals and foliage than the old. Blooms are single and range from dazzling pure white to various pinks to near true blue. No summer garden should be without them. They are not fussy about soil, but do not thrive in overly wet or dry soil. Growth habit is upright with a dense slender-branched form. They grow to 10 feet high and from 6 to 7 feet wide. Deciduous foliage is bright green, unevenly serrated. They are well suited to a dense hedge or screen; and because they are sterile there is no problem with self-seeding. Here are some new varieties: 'Diana,' large, pure white with hundreds of blooms, each lasting more than a day. This variety is sterile and does not self-seed everywhere. Hybridizers are working on other sterile varieties, which should be on the market soon. Other new varieties that offer eye-catching new colors are 'Aphrodite,' deep rose-pink with a showy deep red eye; 'Helene,' pure white with a deep reddish-purple eye; 'Minerva,' lavender-pink with a reddish-purple eye and ruffled petals; 'Blue Bird,' a single bloom in a wonderful blue color.

Hydrangeas These spectacular old-fashioned flowers are staging a dramatic comeback, with many new hybrids introduced each year. They are evocative of lazy summer afternoons of yore, of lemonade, ice cream socials, and golf croquet on green grass. They prefer rich, moist, well-drained soil and are easy to grow. Blue or pink blossom color depends on acid or alkaline soil. Acid soil results in blue; alkaline produces pink, rose, or red. If you want blue flowers, apply Miracid to the soil in spring, according to the directions on the package. If you want pink, rose, or red flowers, work about ½ cup of lime into the soil around the plant. Hydrangeas are very easily propagated. Just take cuttings in the fall, stick them in the ground, and by spring you'll have new plants. Here are some varieties you can select from:

Hydrangea macrophylla (garden or big-leaf hydrangea) A handsome rounded-form variety from 4 to 6 feet high, with upright branches. Green foliage has serrated margins. Enormous pom-pom clusters of blossoms in deep blue or pale pink, depending on soil. Prune to about 2 feet when growth starts in spring, cutting just above an emerging bud. Thrives in sun to shade.

H. paniculata 'Grandiflora' (peegee hydrangea) Tall-growing, to 10 to 15 feet by 8 to 10 feet wide. They are utterly spectacular in late summer when covered with 12- to 18-inch-long by 6- to 12-inch-wide flower clusters. These open white and turn to a coppery pink. Green foliage also changes to a colorful yellow in autumn. Likes sun or shade.

H. quercifolia (oak-leaf hydrangea) Splendid tough plant with dark green, oak leaf-shaped leathery foliage and, in midsummer, elongated panicles of large pure

At sunset, the light illuminates the high-pruned bark of the ornamental tree while *Hydrangea* 'Pink Pygmy' blooms beneath. The golden grass is *Hoconechloa* 'Aurea,' and *Impatiens* 'Neon Salmon' and *Hosta* 'Gold Bullion' add contrast to the planting.

white blooms that slowly turn to a pale pink. Grows 5 to 7 feet high with a similar spread. Thrives in both deep shade and full sun. A sensational plant for any garden.

H. 'Variegata' (variegated lace-cap hydrangea) One of the most beautiful of the hydrangeas is this delicate, deciduous shrub that thrives in shade. Blossoms are of the lace-cap genre, with blue flowers in the center and white on the perimeter. Foliage is vividly edged with white. Flowers bloom from midsummer to fall and grow to about 4 feet. Prefers moist acidic soil. Prune lightly to shape and to keep in bounds.

Lagerstroemia indica (crape myrtle) These wonderful accents for the late-summer garden offer long-lasting clusters of crinkly crepe-like colorful blooms, with handsome green, deciduous foliage that turns golden bronze in the fall. They prefer well-drained, moist soil that is rich in organic matter, so remember to add substantial amounts of compost, rotted manure, or sphagnum peat moss to the planting soil. There are many varieties, some of which are the size of small trees. Prune only to keep in bounds.

Here in our eastern Long Island garden, which is in Zone 7A, we continually try to stretch zone recommendations. We have done it with camellias, both japonica and sasanqua, with great success. These are generally considered to be hardy only to Zone 8 and iffy in Zone 7.

Different varieties of crape myrtle grow from a dwarf 3 feet high to a towering, tree-like 15 feet. Dwarf varieties are better suited to the garden. The dwarf varieties grow from 3 to 5 feet high by about 4 feet wide. Their rich green foliage has a bronze tint when it first emerges in spring. Here are some recommended varieties: rose-red Petite Embers 'Moners,' dark orchid Petite Orchid 'Monhid,' clear pink Petite Pinkie 'Monkie,' deep plum-purple–colored Petite Plum 'Monum,' deep crimson Petite Red Imp 'Monimp,' and snow-white Petite Snow 'Monow.' Tall growers are dark purple 'Catawba' (15 feet); rich red 'Cherokee' (9 feet); white 'Glendora' (25 feet); 'Near East' (15 to 20 feet); 'Peppermint Lace' (15 to 20 feet).

L. indica x *faurieri* hybrids (crape myrtle) Slightly more hardy are these two varieties: clear medium pink 'Pecos' (8 feet high by 5 feet wide) and dark lavender 'Zuni' (9 feet high by 8 feet wide). You can try these in sheltered areas in Zone 6.

Magnolia grandiflora 'Little Gem' About ten years ago, we put in a new variety of the classic southern *Magnolia grandiflora* called 'Little Gem.' Up to that time, there were no dwarf varieties available. The classics grow to 80 or 90 feet, far too large for our garden. We

This *Hydrangea* 'Glowing Embers' takes on its deep blue or purple color because the soil is acid. If the soil is alkaline, the hydrangea would be pink. By adding Miracid to the soil for blue or lime for pink, you can make sure hydrangeas are the color you want. In either case the effect is always stunning and so evocative of another era.

93

We waited seven years for our 'Little Gem' magnolia to bloom. We say that the waiting period was Scarlet's Revenge. It was well worth the wait for now it blooms at three different times during the summer and is covered with these enormous, heavily scented blooms.

waited and waited, year in and year out, and had about given up on ever seeing those enormous, sweet-smelling southern magnolia blossoms. Finally, in the eighth year, we had four glorious blooms in August. Each subsequent year there have been more and more blooms, which open sporadically from around July fourth through the beginning of September. Patience, in this case, paid off handsomely. The tree has reached its mature height now, about 20 feet. The glistening green leaves have a deep bronze coloring beneath. And the large, cup-shaped, fragrant white flowers are a full-scale spectacle in our garden.

Spiraea x *bumalda* 'Limemound' (dwarf pink bridal wreath) is truly a plant for all seasons. Early in the spring, the emerging lemon yellow foliage sports a russet tinge. As the season progresses, the foliage turns lime green. And then in late summer, light pink blossoms cover the plant. In autumn the foliage becomes orange-red on red stems. Now, I'd say that's quite an order for any plant to fill. It is tough as nails, is not fussy about soil, hardy as far north as Zone 3, and pretty to look at. As a bonus, it often sends up new shoots that can be dug up and treated as separate plants or given to friends. Prune only to shape the plant.

Vitex agnus-castus (chaste tree) Vitex grows rapidly to 10 to 20 feet, but can be kept in bounds by selective pruning. Its deciduous foliage is gray-green with silvery white undersides, palm-shaped, and aromatic. Fragrant, 3- to 6-inch clusters of bluish-purple flowers cover the tree from mid- to late summer. Winter bark is corky and chunky in appearance. Vitex is not fussy about soil and thrives in average garden soil. There is only one variety available. Prune to keep in bounds.

Besides attracting birds all during the year, you will want to add the charm of butterflies to your garden. Since many natural butterfly habitats have been lost to urbanization and development, some environmental organizations have incorporated butterfly conservation into their programs. *Buddleia* (butterfly bush), mentioned above, is one of the best plants used to attract butterflies. But there are many other plants that also serve to attract them.

Here are some annuals to plant to attract butterflies: ageratum, common sunflower, cosmos, globe candytuft, gomphrena, heliotrope, lantana, marigold, nasturtium, nicotiana, petunia, salvia, scabiosa, snapdragon, statice, sweet alyssum, verbena, and zinnia. Biennials include dame's rocket, wild Queen Anne's lace, and thistle. Herbs are catnip, chives, dill, lavender, mint, parsley, and sweet fennel. Perennials are allium, aster, bee balm, butterfly weed, chrysanthemum, coneflower, coreopsis, daylily, gaillardia, goldenrod, hollyhock, joe-pye weed, liatris, mallow, milkweed, phlox, pinks, pussy-toes, rudbeckia, sedum, Shasta daisy, veronica, and yarrow.

We do continue to feed the birds during the summer, but only use the thistle feeder to attract goldfinches, which add such beauty to the garden. Through the years, our garden has become a bird sanctuary, and many different varieties of birds build their nests and rear their young in the garden. Hummingbirds are a favorite. They are attracted by bright red and tubular flowers, such as *Crocosmia* 'Lucifer,' red zinnias, lilies, nicotiana, and petunias. Hummingbird feeders do work for some, but we have found that their natural food supply, the nectar of flowers, is the most reliable lure.

Even though summer is a time to relax and enjoy the garden, there are still chores that must be tended to. Beyond the usual mowing of grass and weeding, August is the time to plant iris and peonies. If your window boxes look a little ratty, start thinking about changing the display for the fall garden. Small chrysanthemum plants are readily available and can be planted at the end of summer for fall bloom. If you grow roses, and other plants as well, summer is the time when Japanese beetles arrive. Here are a few words about them sent to me by an old friend, the Reverend Norman Strauss, who grows roses in upstate New York: "Thank goodness! They say the J. beetles leave in the middle of August to go back to the earth where they manufacture grubs, where one can spray Grub Killer and Milky Spore and whatever else to get rid of them for next year. I am so sick and tired of picking them off the roses and either squeezing them to death or dropping them in a jar of soapy water. I wish they would go back to the land of the rising sun. I've even drawn a rising sun on the soapy water jar but I doubt if they get the message before they get . . . *the message* . . . glub, blub."

Autumn is our favorite time of the year in our garden. Usually the skies are a clear blue, the sun shines almost daily, sunsets are painted with intense colors of orange, screaming pink, and red that bathe the garden in these loveliest of fall colors. The air has become fresh and chilly, and the garden puts on its fall and perhaps most beautiful spectacle. On the North Fork, leaves begin to turn around the middle of October and remain on the trees until mid-November. Each day the colors become more and more intense. At night, the moon takes on the cold, clear winter look.

Now is another time for leisurely strolls through the garden, romping in the piles of fallen leaves with Mr. Chips, picking chrysanthemums and autumn foliage for indoor flower arrangements, and not worrying too much about the garden being tidy. The property here is surrounded by many very large, old trees. There is an elm, one of the few surviving on Long Island, that sports yellow leaves. The Norway maples are brilliant gold, the sugar maple is a deep red. Hundred-year-old copper beeches turn bronze, locusts and birches yellow, and our fences, which are covered with Boston ivy, turn a spectacular brilliant red and stay that way for about two weeks, after which they too lose their leaves. We did try using Virginia creeper, the American native vine that turns a beautiful red in the fall; however, it is very invasive and given a few years would probably bring down not only the

fence but the house. Boston ivy is very tidy and is easily kept under control. The various clematis that are scattered throughout the garden also offer their feathery seedpods. However, *Clematis* 'Bill McKenzie' is in its late-blooming glory, covered with delicate yellow blossoms.

Since the area is still essentially a farm community, all over the North Fork, people decorate their houses for the fall harvest. Pumpkins, corn stalks, and pots and pots of chrysanthemums are everywhere. The hydrangea flowers have turned from pink or blue to a rich autumn bronze. The farm stands are filled with the last of the summer vegetables and autumn's cauliflower, pumpkins, winter squash, broccoli, potatoes, Indian corn, Brussels sprouts, cabbage, and beets. The evenings grow longer, the chimneys have been cleaned, and firewood and kindling for the fires are handy. We invite friends over for bourbon old-fashioneds and backgammon. Along with the daily evening fire, we use only natural light in the living room; that is, only light from candles and oil lamps. After all, the house is a 260-year-old landmark, and historical societies all over the country feature candlelight tours around the holidays, so we have one of our own. Why not enjoy it every evening?

Squirrels are busy at this time of the year. They go back and forth all day long between

With the arrival of fall, the country roads of the North Fork dazzle with the autumn foliage. The similar climatic conditions make the display as colorful as that in New England.

We have flanked the gate leading to the perennial garden with the old reliable *Sedum* 'Autumn Joy.' The pink blossom clusters will turn to brilliant rust as the season progresses. The purple flowering shrub on the right is a crape myrtle, which is hardy on the East End of Long Island. ▓ Our regal North Fork swans glide elegantly by the golden autumn grasses of the wetlands.

The plants in this part of the garden put on quite a show in early fall. Included are chrysanthemums, Japanese anemones, and Michaelmas daisies. The tall, white-blooming shrub is Althaea (hibiscus) 'Diane,' which blooms throughout the summer and into the fall. It is sterile so does not leave nuisance seedlings all over the place like most other althaeas.

Clockwise from left: By the dawn's early light, this *Euonymus alata* (burning bush or winged euonymus) sparkles in the mist and complements the straw-colored ornamental grass in the foreground. ■ The *Parthenocissus* (Boston ivy) on our stockade fence has already turned brilliant red. Yellow *Datura* (angel's trumpets) grow in the container that we purposely move to this location in the fall. ■ After they bloom in late spring or summer, all clematis bear these fluffy seedpods that remain on the plant until late fall. ■ *Clematis* 'Bill McKenzie,' a yellow variety, is one of the last to bloom, often flowering into October.

Since traditionally the North Fork has always been an agricultural community, residents decorate porches and gardens with corn stalks, pumpkins, chrysanthemums, and flowering kale to celebrate the harvest season. ▩ Here is another harvest decoration, set in front of a hydrangea bush. Hydrangea blooms turn a beautiful purple-bronze in the fall and can be cut and used in dry flower arrangements for the house.

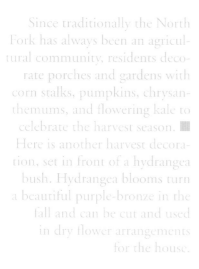

In the fall, fields of pumpkins on farms all over the North Fork decorate the landscape. Particularly on weekends, day-trippers come out by the thousands from "up-island" to buy their Halloween pumpkins. ▮ The farmers grow Indian corn for the fall season. Many people hang a clump of it on their back doors as well as their front. The tradition of visitors using the back door persists here. In fact, our front door has not been opened since we moved a piano into the house nine years ago.

the copper beeches that surround the house, gathering nuts and burying them. Since the entire garden is enclosed by a stockade fence, they love to race along the top of the fence from one end to the other. And the geese start to fly back and forth over the house in formation, honking their fool heads off and causing Mr. Chips to get all excited and crane his neck to see them. Like suburban commuters, they are very predictable because they go in one direction during the morning and then return in late afternoon, day in and day out. Swans gather in the creeks in the fall, setting up their winter colonies. In the spring when they nest, they are not very communal; in fact, they are viciously territorial and prefer to hatch and raise their cygnets off somewhere by themselves.

The birds are out in droves, eating berries off all the shrubs and trees planted to attract them. Many are preparing for the long flight south. At this time of year pine siskins, Carolina wrens, summer tanagers, and a few lingering warblers are still here. Robins and catbirds will be gone in a week or so. Our 'Snowflake' dogwood is planted directly outside of the windows on the south side of the house. In the fall, it is covered with brilliant red berries. The robins, catbirds, and mockingbirds all love them, and many unusual birds are attracted to them. In fact, as I sit here at the window in my office and write this, I am looking out over the garden and the dogwood, and there are three evening grosbeaks feeding. Their brilliant yellow, black, and white plumage stands out against the burgundy leaves of the dogwood.

As fall unfolds, the fall-blooming perennials put on their annual display. Michaelmas

This planting of white Michaelmas daisies (fall asters) provides bright contrast to the rust of the *Sedum* 'Autumn Joy' and the green of the surrounding plants. ▩ Here's a snappy combination for a fall garden. The delicate blossoms of these pink Japanese anemones are set off by the velvety gray-green foliage of *Stachys* (lamb's ears). ▩ *Imperata cylindrica* 'Red Baron' (Japanese blood grass), with its deep red coloration, is a perfect plant for the fall garden.

daisies, those charming purple, pink, blue, and white fall asters, add their delicate touches to the landscape. Various sedums, like 'Autumn Joy,' don their pink cluster blooms that turn a deep rust as the season progresses. Japanese anemones are all over the place. These attractive pink, or white, or double-rose tall flowers add subtle pastel touches to the otherwise brilliant landscape. On the East End, a type of chrysanthemum called "Montauk daisy" is very popular with gardeners. They resemble the common white daisy, but are not hardy in colder areas. They have naturalized along the beaches in some areas. The story of how they got here is that while they were being brought into the country on a Japanese ship many years ago, the ship hit a violent storm, sank, and the Montauk daisies all drifted onto the beaches and naturalized. Whether or not the story is true, I do not know. From there, locals moved them into gardens, and they offer a stunning daisy display every fall. Wild goldenrod blooms in the fields along with wild purple asters. A hybrid goldenrod colors the garden with brilliant gold. With the colored foliage as a backdrop, the intense bright yellows, reds, and oranges all are appropriate in the garden at this time of year. The fountain grass and miscanthus, along with other grasses, show off their fall inflorescences, the feathery seedpods that they develop through the season, and their foliage begins to turn to its autumn, light creamy-tan color.

Of course, the traditional fall standbys are chrysanthemums, and you can't have enough

103

Clockwise from top left: Most people plant the pom-pom varieties of chrysanthemums for fall. Don't overlook the daisy varieties because they offer an interesting contrast to the usual selections. ■ The elegant inflorescenses of *Miscanthus sinensis* dress up any autumn garden. Don't cut them off because they will persist through the winter and are quite beautiful when the garden is covered with snow. ■ Here is a surefire combination for the fall season. *Pennisetum alopecuroides* (fountain grass), *Sedum* 'Autumn Joy,' and the brilliant blue plumbago look stunning together. ■ In our perennial garden, graceful *Pennisetum alopecuroides* (fountain grass), Japanese anemones, and lingering annual cosmos offer a color combination totally different from that of the same garden in spring and summer.

of them. Their brilliant-colored mounds of flowers echo the colors of the fall foliage: yellow, orange, red, white, purple. They are very inexpensive, perhaps a few dollars apiece. Use them to dress up your window boxes, entranceways, perennial borders, anywhere you want a brilliant splash of fall color. They bloom right through to a deep killing frost. You can plant them in the ground, and they will rebloom the following year since they are perennials and very hardy, but because they are so very inexpensive, just throw them out when they are spent and buy new ones each year. Of late, a lot of people are decorating their houses

These delicate Michaelmas daisies (fall asters) form an impressive mound of purple color in the fall garden. Although very few people grow them and have yet to discover them, we love them and keep adding more to the garden every year. ▦ For an instant fall fix in the garden, you can't beat chrysanthemums. They are quite inexpensive and readily available all over the country. Use them wherever you want a brilliant dash of color.

and gardens with colorful kale, which is available in red, fuchsia, yellow, green, and purple. We tend not to use them because they are somewhat garish but if used in moderation, they do look reasonably good. And if you don't like them, you can make a fine soup out of them.

The annual marigolds, petunias, and others are still in bloom, but our favorite is the new *Calibrachoa* (million bells), the pink, blue, white, or yellow petunia-like mounds of flowers, which never stop blooming. Next year there will be a great many more in the garden, because they dress it up until a killing frost.

About two years after I bought my house and started my garden, my mother was visiting. It was a gorgeous fall day, the skies were clear blue, and the trees were dressed in full autumn foliage. We were unaware that we were about to witness one of nature's extraordinary spectacles. As I walked around in the garden, I noticed that there were about ten monarch butterflies circling around above. I didn't take any heed of it, butterflies were frequent visitors. About fifteen minutes later, there were hundreds of them, their brilliant rust color contrasting with the leaves in the surrounding tall maple trees. I went inside to get my mother, and told her about the strange occurrence. We both went outside to watch. As time wore on, more and more butterflies were swirling around in the garden. There were thousands, and within half an hour, probably hundreds of thousands of them had settled in on the maple trees, I expected, to spend the night. The entire tree was a dazzling mass of rust-orange fluttering butterfly wings. We had witnessed one of nature's great spectacles; that is, the migration of the monarch butterflies to Mexico, where they go every year for the winter. There had been a fresh shower just before our first sightings, and a double rainbow arched through the heavens. Alas, I had no camera, and couldn't find anyone at home with one so it is all a memory, as clear as a bell in my mind, but still a memory. It was, of course, a once in a lifetime experience, and I know it will never happen again. But I have seen one of nature's truly spectacular events, and it happened right here in our garden.

There are also times in the garden that are not quite as aesthetic and tranquil as viewing the butterfly migration. The fall is also the time when violent hurricanes churn up the

waters and devastate coastal areas in their path. Nature has been kind during the past twenty years, for only two major hurricanes have passed through our area: Gloria and Bob. When Gloria paid us a visit, the Weather Bureau had warned early in the morning that the winds could well top 120 miles per hour by 11:00 A.M. At that intensity, roofs fly off houses. Mercifully, although the storm caused a great deal of damage and there was no power for over a week, the brunt of it did not come ashore here. Three trees were lost, a very tall green birch, half of an old balsam, and an ancient pear. Frankly, all three were quite old and were really in the wrong places in what was becoming our own garden so it was not a great calamity. The ancient yew stood fast and didn't even lose a limb.

But we did learn that some of our ornamental trees are more susceptible to splintering than others. The limbs of franklinia trees are especially prone to snapping off during heavy winds. So among the many other chores that must be done before heavy storms, we hammered some metal stakes in the ground around ours and then tried as best we could to wrap ropes around the tree and tie them to the stakes. Although during the height of the storm, the tree was straining mightily to break its bonds, it nonetheless did not and so was spared damage. Dogwoods also will split, as will any ornamental that has a forked trunk. You can avoid this by training your ornamentals to a single trunk when they are young. Then, in the event of a storm, two sturdy stakes and very tight roping usually saves the tree from damage.

Mirrors, which we use a lot in the garden, were removed, barn and cellar doors secured, summer furniture brought into the barn, garden ornaments stored away, and bird feeders

We recently discovered annual *Calibrachoa* (million bells). They look like tiny petunias and bloom their heads off from June until a killing frost. This plant is in our rock garden, and we use it in urns as well. They are tough, drought resistant, and, most important, you do not have to deadhead them in order to keep them blooming. ■ Moonflowers keep blooming until late fall. Here are some on an arch leading from our brick courtyard to a small garden area. We placed a number of potted chrysanthemums in front of them to add some fall color.

taken down. In short, anything that might fly off a wall or tree had to be put away or tied down. Batteries, flashlights, transistor radios, gallons of water, and canned foods were laid in. In anticipation of a power outage and in case it turned chilly, wood was stacked up on the porch so that a journey back to the woodpile through the inevitable debris that would collect during the storm would be unnecessary. We also brought some wood inside the house and put it in the kitchen. While sitting waiting for the storm, suddenly, and with no apparent reason, Sasha, our late beagle, was barking his head off. I said, "Sasha is barking. Something is wrong." Harry said, "Sasha always barks, nothing is wrong." I said, "But it's a different kind of bark." I went into the kitchen and lo and behold, along with the wood, there was a snake, which, like Sister Kate and Gilda Gray, was dancing the shimmy across the oak floor. Of course Sasha was barking. Now here's a tip if you ever have an errant snake in your house. And don't forget it. Just take a large bath towel and throw it over the snake, wrap it up, take it outside, and release it. If you ever find a snake in your house, you will be very grateful that you know how to get rid of the problem.

Another time during a storm, a bird flew down the chimney. When the terrified bird settled down a bit, I simply put a hat over him, then slowly worked the hat over a large piece of cardboard. Then I left the hat on the bird, which was on the cardboard, went outdoors, and released him. Remember this as well, because one day you will be grateful that you know how to do it for there is nothing quite so unnerving as having a helpless bird desperately flying around your house trying to get out.

Northeast storms, which can be quite violent and destructive, also pass through this part of the world, usually from late summer to winter. Although they are not as devastating as hurricanes, the same precautions should be taken. Years ago, before brown tide decimated our local scallop larder, after a northeast storm, everyone would go down to the beach at dawn, before the gulls got to them, and just pick hundreds of scallops that had washed up on the beach.

All gardeners tend to relax and enjoy the garden during the summer moths. All the spring planting has been done, the garden is showing off its various spectacles, and so we revel in what we have created. But come fall, there are chores that must be tended to. First, fall is planting time. All spring-blooming bulbs, as well as most autumn-blooming bulbs, must be planted in the fall. It is also the best time to plant or move shrubs or small trees. This is because, unlike in the spring, the top growth has stopped and all of the energy goes into establishing the root structure of the plant. Projects, of course, are a part of any garden. And during the hot summer months, we put them off, and with good reason. Who wants to start a major project in the blistering heat and humidity of August?

Once the display of foliage is over, all of those fallen leaves must be raked up, bagged, and disposed of or turned into compost. I remember as a child how we all used to roll around in the piles of leaves with our puppy. And there was that wonderful smell of burning leaves everywhere. It was a nice smell, which to this day brings to mind the tangy taste of cider and doughnuts. But environmental concerns have done away with most of that. Out here on the East End, because there are too many leaves to compost, we bag the leaves and brush and take them to the dump.

Spent perennials must be cut back to discourage disease that might be harbored in the decaying foliage over the winter. Overgrown perennials should be divided now. Be sure to give any excess to fellow gardeners or friends. Invite them over and visit for a while and catch up on things. Bald spots in the lawn or in ground-cover areas should be filled in and reseeded now. And late fall is the time when you prune most shrubs. Stand back, take a good hard look at shrubs and ornamental trees, and then decide which limbs you want to remove. Usually one of two crisscrossing limbs is removed. Too many forks in a tree's structure can lead to major splits during fall hurricanes or winter storms. We always wait to prune our evergreens and hollies of any foliage that could be useful in decorating during the holidays. If you don't have a holly bush in your garden, go out and buy one now and plant it. Then next year, you will have all of that holly foliage and berries to decorate your house. And if you have the space for balsam or white pine, plant those as well. They are invaluable as holiday decorations. Garden furniture, ornaments, and lighting must all be taken out of the garden and stored inside a shed, barn, or garage.

Check all bird feeders once again to see that they do not need repair and that they are clean. And start to feed the birds again if you have stopped during the summer. Remember that if you want to attract goldfinches to your garden, they like thistle or Niger seed, and if you want to feed them, you must get a special thistle feeder, which all garden centers offer. A suet feeder filled with beef fat, which most butchers will gladly give you for nothing, is another good idea for this attracts woodpeckers, titmice, chickadees, and nuthatches.

In our garden, the pond must also be put to sleep. We net the pond when the leaves begin to fall so that they don't go into the water and foul it. Some plants, such as lotus, must be lowered into the deepest part of the pond in order to survive the winter. The pump and mechanism are removed for the winter and stored away. The fish are usually just fine through the winter. As I understand it, they all go down to the bottom of the pond where there is a wet bar and hang out there. Frogs burrow in the mud and sleep through the cold.

Because our winters are quite mild, almost all of the fish survive. However, once in a while we do lose a few. It is important that there be a hole in the top of the pond ice if it covers the entire pond. This is so that noxious gases can escape and oxygen can get into the pond. And never take a hammer and bang a hole in the ice as it can give the fish concussions. There is a simple heating device available which is put on top of the pond and turned on when ice forms. This melts a small hole on the iced surface and allows for the exchange of fresh air and foul gases.

As you read in Chapter Two, Spring in the Garden, fall is the time to plant spring-blooming bulbs. All information regarding spring bulbs is included in that chapter. However, there is a whole class of bulbs that you plant in late summer or early fall that bloom within several weeks. These are called the fall bulbs, and many are autumn versions of our spring crocuses. They add charming touches to any garden if for no other reason than that they look just like spring species crocus. Naturalized in woodland areas, where one tends to wander in the fall amid the fallen red and yellow leaves, they are quite attractive.

Most spring-blooming bulbs can be planted as long as the soil is workable. Tulips are best if not planted until November. And in fact, I have known of people who didn't get around to planting their daffodils and so just put them in the basement in a bucket, where they sprouted later. They were planted but did not bloom that year, but the following year, they bloomed along with those planted in the fall. All autumn-blooming bulbs are hardy to Zone 3. And since all autumn-blooming bulbs are dormant in summer, they are drought-resistant. Here are some we like:

Autumn Crocus have small, elegant cup-shaped blooms 4 to 6 inches high in rose, pink, blue, violet, and yellow over grass-like foliage. Plant in August or September. Set out in full sun or partial shade, pointed end up, 3 to 4 inches deep and 2 inches apart in light, well-drained, somewhat sandy soil. Many perennialize. It is a good idea to work in a handful of bonemeal around the planting in late summer every year. Varieties include:

Cassiope	Pale lilac, with a white center
Kotschyanus	Deep rose pink
Kotschyanus Albus	Pure white
C. sativus	Lilac with orange stems
Speciosus	Pale lilac with darker edges

Colchicum come in single and double varieties in deep lilac, lavender, pure white, and rose pink. They look like big crocus, on 4- to 8-inch stems over large glossy leaves. Plant in late summer or early fall

Annual white sweet alyssum almost always reseeds itself every year and provides a lovely foreground for this planting of fall-blooming *Colchicum* in our friend Roberta Lee's garden. Although most people are not aware of them, there are many varieties of fall crocus in white, blue, or purple that are readily available through mail-order houses.

for fall bloom. Set corms in full sun or semishade in soil fortified with peat moss, 3 inches deep, 4 to 6 inches apart. Maintain even moisture until blooming ends. Varieties include:

The Giant	**Large, deep lilac flowers**
Double Water Lily	**Lavender-pink**
C. Autumnale Album	**Pure white**
C. Cilicicum	**Rosy pink**
C. Speciosum	**Soft lavender-pink with a white center**

Sternbergia have bright yellow, crocus-like blossoms after long strap-shaped leaves die in summer. They then flower until frost on plants 6 to 8 inches tall. Plant bulbs in early fall in full sun, 4 to 6 inches apart, 1 inch deep, in dry, very well-drained, heavy soil. They will perennialize and multiply readily. One planting here now covers several square feet. They are great favorites, and every year we plant more.

Almost all of the major floral and shrub displays are over for the year by fall, and as the weeks go by, fewer and fewer flowers will be in bloom in the garden. But the change of color of the autumn foliage is indeed a spectacle, perhaps the most lavish of the year, and with proper selection of various cultivars, you can enhance nature's exhibition with touches of your own. If you look around your neighborhood and adjoining property, you will probably see a Norway maple or two. They turn brilliant gold in the fall. Oak trees turn bright red or coppery red. Birches, gingko, and elm trees also turn various shades of yellow. But the shrubs and ornamental trees that you plant in your garden with fall foliage in mind are

Fall-blooming, yellow *Sternbergia*, also bulbs, look quite disarming poking their heads up through the brilliant-colored fall leaves of autumn. ▓ This rose-purple crape myrtle is one of fall's most beautiful blooming shrubs. But, alas, they are only hardy to Zone 7A. So all of you folks in chillier areas will have to be content just looking at pictures of them. ▓ This very special rock garden is all dressed up for fall with straw-colored grasses and flowering heath. Notice how the blue-green and bright green dwarf evergreens add such an elegant touch of texture, color, and form to the landscape.

the stars of this spectacle. As a bonus, many of these brilliantly fall-foliated shrubs offer flowers earlier in the season and berries later in the winter. Here are some you should include in your garden:

Abelia x *grandiflora* (glossy abelia) is a late-blooming deciduous shrub with pinkish-white flowers in late summer and fall on finely textured, glossy, elegant, arching deep green foliage that turns bronze in fall. It grows to 4 feet and thrives in well-drained soil, in semi-shade to full sun, and with average moisture.

Acer palmatum dissectum (looseleaf Japanese maple) is a deciduous, slow-growing dwarf tree, used as a shrub, sporting soft, wispy foliage. They are many shades of red and green, some with variegated leaves. They grow from 6 to 8 feet and thrive in well-drained, acid soil rich in organic matter, in filtered shade with protection from heavy winds. The autumn foliage of many varieties is spectacular yellow, red, and combinations thereof. Try to find the dwarf varieties so that you can plant more of them in your garden. There are six different varieties in ours, one more beautiful than the next.

Aronia arbutifolia 'Brilliantissima' (chokeberry) is a splendid, compact, deciduous shrub that has white flowers in spring, followed in autumn by long-lasting glossy red berries and leaves. It is beautiful massed along a pathway in a woodland grove or in a large perennial or shrub border.

Berberis thunbergii (Japanese barberry) is a deciduous shrub. Most produce pinkish or reddish new leaves in late spring that turn to green or burgundy in summer, then color orange, yellow, and red in fall. Small attractive yellow flowers bloom in midspring, but are usually hidden to a great extent by the foliage. In late summer, red-purplish or blue-black fruits appear that later turn brilliant red, complementing the fall foliage colors of red, yellow, purple, and dark green. They grow from 2 to 5 feet. Sandy soil is adequate and they are drought-resistant. Barberry is a compact, thorny shrub often used for hedges because it takes pruning well. The thorns tend to collect debris, which can be difficult to remove. Plant some deep red climbing roses, such as 'Blaze,' in tandem with barberry for a dazzling display.

Betula nigra (river birch) and *B. utilis jacquemontii* (Himalayan birch) are two varieties of birch that are not attacked by birch miner, which if left unchecked will kill a birch tree. The river birch has been hybridized so that there is now a gorgeous white-barked dwarf variety that grows to only 8 to 10 feet. Most birches grow to fifty feet. Himalayan birch is the most elegant of all the birches, with snow-white bark and deep rust-mahogany underbark. Both are worth searching for since they are not offered by most nurseries and mail-order houses. Fairweather Gardens in New Jersey offers the dwarf river birch and Forest Farm in Oregon offers the Himalayan birch. I have not seen them anywhere else.

Buxus (boxwood) is a broad-leafed evergreen shrub. The traditional shrub for hedges, tightly branched, with small lustrous leaves, it grows from 18 inches to 6 feet depending on the variety, of which there are many in cultivation. Boxwood thrives in sun or partial shade and in ordinary soil and is drought resistant once established. Dwarf forms are ideal for edging beds. Some people object to the dank odor that boxwood puts forth on humid days in summer while to others they are the apotheosis of any garden shrub, revered for centuries.

Camellia japonica and *C. sasanqua* are broad-leafed evergreen shrubs, and we consider ourselves extremely fortunate to be able to grow them on the East End of Long Island. They do not offer brilliantly colored foliage, but a deep glossy green mantle. The *C. japonica* bloom in the spring in glorious pink, red, white, and now even pale yellow colors on glossy elegant foliage. But in the late fall and into early winter, the *C. sasanqua* bloom with single and double white, red, or pink flowers and combinations thereof, adding glorious color to the early winter garden. Our 'Snowflake' *sasanqua* blooms at Christmas. They are vigorous plants so you must be careful where you plant them. Most grow 6 to 15 feet. They are usually inappropriate for foundation plantings or in smaller shrub borders. Despite what most people think, they are not fussy plants at all. Except when it comes to extreme cold, of course, since they are only hardy to Zone 7B. They thrive in ordinary soil, even heavy soil that is fortified with organic matter and slightly acid. They prefer partial to deep shade, not full sun, because the sun burns the blossoms in spring and the foliage in summer. They do not like southern exposure.

Chamaecyparis (false cypress) is a conifer, and you must always remember that the evergreen foliage of these plants adds considerable beauty to any fall or winter landscape. They come in many different shapes and colors. Some are globular, others pyramidal or spreading, in silver, blue, green, or gold foliage depending on the variety. Always use dwarf varieties unless you have a very large piece of property because they will not overpower your landscape. Recommended dwarf varieties include:

C. obtusa 'Nana Aurea' (dwarf gold Hinoki cypress) Heavy gold foliage.

C. obtusa 'Kosteri Nana' Lacy foliage, broad growth habit.

C. obtusa 'Torulosa Nana' (dwarf twisted-branch cypress) Branches are twisted; compact irregular pyramidal form.

Opposite: Acer palmatum 'Sango kaku' (coral bark maple) is one of the most desirable plants you can have in your garden. It delivers beauty in spring, summer, fall, and winter. In spring, the new leaves are a bright green, bordered with yellow. In summer, foliage is medium green. In fall, it is bright yellow and orange, and in winter the bark of the tree turns a brilliant red. If you have room for one small tree, go with this one. ■
Callicarpa (beauty berry) is a native American plant and the only one in the world that sports these bright purple berries. They are useful to dress up shrub borders for fall displays.

Our friend Alice Levien has planted pink-flowering *Sedum* 'Autumn Joy' to contrast with the bright red berries of this Korean dogwood. The berries are edible, and apparently some people make jelly out of them, but we have tasted them and as far as we are concerned, they are strictly for the birds. ▥ Yellow button chrysanthemums and the variegated foliage of a *C. florida* (dogwood) combine well in this planting. When you plan your fall garden, don't forget to take advantage of foliage colors when selecting flowering annuals and perennials to plant around them. ▥ Behind our little barn is a *Cornus florida* (dogwood), which has just begun to show the change from summer green to fall burgundy. Believe it or not, we found this tree when it was just a seedling, along with about thirty others, beneath an existing dogwood.

C. pisifera 'Argentea Nana' (dwarf silver cypress) Soft plumed silvery-blue foliage; dense globular growth habit. 'Argentea Variegata Anna' has variegated foliage.

C. pisifera 'Aurea Pendula' (dwarf gold thread cypress) Bright golden pendulous filaments; dense low-growing shrub. Does not burn in the sun.

C. pisifera 'Minima' (dwarf threadleaf cypress) Green foliage; compact growth habit.

C. pisifera 'Sulfuria Nana' (dwarf sulfur cypress) Bright sulfur-colored foliage; broad growth habit.

C. pisifera 'Filifera Aurea Variegata Nana' (dwarf gold variegated cypress) Gold variegated foliage.

Cornus florida (dogwood) is a tree for all seasons, offering glorious pink, red, or white blossoms in spring, lustrous green foliage in summer, and brilliant red berries and deep red-burgundy foliage in the fall. Try to locate hybrids that have been developed to resist anthracnose, the fungal disease that has killed so many of our native dogwoods. You can't go wrong with this one. Be sure to include several in your land-

scape. Because red berries on dogwood are so favored by birds, there are rarely any left on the tree when winter comes. For this reason they are included here in the fall chapter.

Cotinus coggygria (smoke bush) is a deciduous shrub that sports cloud-like, pink or white blossoms on spectacular purple foliage. The blossoms are gone by fall, but the deep burgundy-purple foliage persists until the leaves fall after a killing frost. It grows from 6 to 25 feet depending on the variety, but you can keep it under control by cutting it back to about 1 foot in late winter or very early spring. The variety with the most intense purple foliage is 'Velvet Cloak.' Smoke bush thrives in ordinary soil, including dry, rocky soil, and full sun, if possible. Once established, it is drought-resistant. It is particularly effective when planted in combination with barberries.

Euonymus alata (burning bush or winged euonymus) is a deciduous shrub, grown for its spectacular cherry-red fall foliage. It is perhaps the number one plant when it comes to fall foliage spectacle. It thrives in ordinary soil, in full sun or heavy shade, and grows from 4 to 20 feet, depending on the variety. Select from the dwarfs since the standards grow too large for most gardens. Burning bush is drought-resistant once established. Locate the plant where it can grow to its full height because pruning creates unattractive broom-like growth. The cultivar 'Compatus' is often sold as a dwarf. It is not. It grows to almost 15 feet. 'Rudy Haag' and 'Anna' grow from 4 to 6 feet, much more manageable for the average garden.

This is one of our favorites. *Cotinus coggygria* (smoke bush) adds its startling deep burgundy-purple foliage to the landscape throughout the growing season. ▓ Here is a close-up of the foliage of the most spectacular fall plant, *Euonymus alata* (burning bush, also called winged euonymus). The plant has nothing to offer but medium green foliage during the rest of the year but come fall, the cherry red leaves are spectacular. If you have room for only one fall foliage plant in your garden, select this.

113

Enkianthus is another plant that is grown almost solely for its rich orange-yellow-red fall foliage. It is a tidy, carefree plant, and if you have space for it, be sure to plant one.

Fothergilla major (large fothergilla) is a deciduous shrub. It offers honey-scented, white blossoms on dark green, pest-free foliage during the summer and in fall produces a brilliantly colorful display of red, orange, yellow, and scarlet. One of the best for the fall, no garden should be without one. It adapts well to many different conditions but prefers acid, well-drained soil in full sun or partial shade. Drought resistant once established. Select the dwarf variety, *Fothergilla gardenii* (dwarf witch alder), which grows from 6 to 8 feet.

Hydrangea quercifolia (oak-leaf hydrangea) is a deciduous shrub. In summer, lacy white flower clusters cover the plant. Leaves are a coarse, clean, deep green, and the plant grows from 6 to 8 feet, but can be pruned to maintain dwarf size. Thrives in moist, slightly acid, fertile, well-drained soil in full sun or semi-shade. In the fall, the foliage turns a deep burgundy color, reasonably rare in the fall foliage selection.

Juniperus (juniper) is a genus of coniferous shrub, like *Chamaecyparis,* and every garden should include some dwarf varieties for textural and color contrast. Creeping, low, and spreading, vase-shaped and columnar, with varying shades of green, blue, or gold foliage. Hardy from Zone 4 to 10, depending on variety. Recommended varieties are:

J. chinensis 'Pfitzeriana Aurea' (gold-tip juniper) Bright golden color in spring and summer.

J. chinensis 'Torulosa' (Hollywood juniper) Dense shrub with twisted branches, to 6 feet.

J. chinensis procumbens 'Nana' (dwarf Japanese juniper or Pronina juniper) Short stiff branches forming a carpet up to 6 feet across, mounding to 10 feet in the center.

J. horizontalis 'Bar Harbor' (Bar Harbor juniper) Creeping form; steel blue foliage with a fern-like appearance.

J. horizontalis 'Plumosa' (Andorra juniper) Low, spreading habit; summer foliage is silvery green, turning purple after frost.

J. horizontalis 'Blue Chip' (blue chip juniper) Silvery-blue foliage, spreading, low, mounding habit.

J. horizontalis 'Glauca' (blue creeping juniper) Creeping form, blue foliage.

J. rigida 'Pendula' (weeping needle juniper) Narrow, tall, and pendant in habit.

Magnolia stellata (star magnolia) is a small deciduous tree. Large white star-shaped blossoms dazzle in early spring. Thrives in deep, rich, well-drained, moist soil in full sun to partial shade. Grows 6 to 20 feet, depending on variety. Select from dwarf varieties that are more in scale with the average garden. Its leathery foliage is particularly attractive in the fall.

Oxydendrum arboreum (sourwood or sorrel tree) is a very slow-growing tree that reaches about 15 to 25 feet after fifteen years or so. Before that, it is a handsome small tree, or large shrub, with magnificent fall foliage in orange and scarlet that later turns to dark purple. In the summer, bell-shaped creamy white blossoms cover the tree. When the foliage turns color in the fall, brilliant branching clusters of greenish seed capsules extend outward and downward like fingers. As the season wears on they turn to light or silver-gray. Sorrel tree likes acid well-drained soil, tolerates some drought, and prefers sun but will grow well in semishade.

Picea abies 'Nidiformis' (bird's-nest spruce) is another useful coniferous shrub. It is a dwarf with delicate needles on a dense, low mound. Thrives in well-drained, sandy soil. Drought resistant, but water during prolonged droughts. Thrives in full sun or partial shade and grows 3 to 6 feet. A fine selection for rock gardens and contrasts well in the fall with deciduous shrubs and trees.

P. glauca 'Conica' (Alberta spruce) is another dwarf member of the spruce family. It is conical, slow-growing, and can be useful in many ways in the landscape. Not fussy about soil, it does equally well in full sun or partial shade. Like its cousin above, it adapts well to rock gardens and at focal points in the garden.

Rhododendron species (Rhododendrons and azaleas) add much to the fall garden. The broad-leafed evergreen varieties retain their deep green luster, but it is the deciduous varieties that turn brilliant red, yellow, orange, or deep purple during the fall. There are hundreds of deciduous varieties, and beyond the brilliant spring display they offer, their autumn foliage is spectacular. The Korean *Rhododendron* 'Cornell Pink' is particularly beautiful in the fall.

Sorbus (mountain ash or rowan) is a small tree that grows to about 30 feet. In the fall, it sports clusters of brilliant orange-red berries. If you have the space, one of these is a fine addition to any garden, but keep in mind, it is a fall spectacle only.

Thuja occidentalis (American arborvitae) is another coniferous native shrub. Pyramidal, conical, globular, and columnar forms with gold and light to dark green foliage. Hardy to Zone 2. Two useful varieties are 'Hetz's Midget' (dwarf globe arborvitae), a slow-growing, globular shrub with medium green foliage and 'Woodwardii' (Woodward globe arborvitae), a bushy shrub that can even be used in window boxes.

The swirling effect of the petals of *Echinacea* (purple coneflower) adds a slightly unruly, wild touch to a fall garden.

Although bright and unlikely color combinations do not suit many gardeners in summer, in the fall these red dahlias and purple *Allium* work so very well with the autumn color ambiance.

Viburnum is a large group of deciduous shrubs with many varieties suitable for the fall garden. Most are planted for their pretty spring blooms, but some offer fall spectacle as well. Recommended varieties include:

V. carlesii (Korean spice viburnum) Waxy fragrant blossoms, tinged pink in early spring on gray-green foliage that turns bronze-red in fall, grows to 6 feet; shapely growth habit.

V. dentatum (arrowwood) A native that adapts to boggy conditions, with attractive clusters of white blossoms in spring, followed by blue berries on deep green foliage which turns bright red in autumn. Grows to 8 to 14 feet.

V. plicatum tomentosum (doublefile viburnum) Lacy, pure white pinwheel blossoms on dark green foliage that turn into red fruit in the fall. It grows from 8 to 10 feet. Many consider this the finest of all viburnums.

Here on the North Fork, Thanksgiving is the end of the fall season. Every year, weather permitting, after dinner with friends, we always spend an hour or so wandering around the garden, knowing that it is probably the last time until spring when an extended walk is comfortable and pleasant. During the following week, our neighbors and friends all start dismantling their autumn displays, to be replaced by Christmas decorations. It is an exciting time, despite the fact that the year in the life of the garden is growing to a close. As soon as they start playing "Jingle Bells" on the radio stations, winter is on its way. And, of course, all of the holiday festivities are perhaps the most wonderful part of every year. But the garden is slowly sinking into deep winter slumber. It will not be until spring that it will once again reward our work, our thoughts, our planning and our dreams with its glorious displays. But there is also beauty in sleep, and our Sleeping Beauty, like the classic ballet, offers very special treats during the winter season.

Fall is the time for drying all manner of plant material for use in dried arrangements in the house or for potpourri or herbs for the kitchen. We dry grasses, blossoms, herbs, and foliage and enjoy them through the winter.

There is a very special beauty about the garden in the winter. The freshly fallen snow and the berry-laden shrubs transform the garden into yet another spectacle, the final one of the garden year. All during the winter on the North Fork, the geese and ducks continue to go back and forth between their daytime and their nighttime habitats. Brussels sprouts and cabbage are still being harvested by the farmers because our winters are quite mild, and it usually doesn't get very cold until after the first of the year. The swans gather on the creeks, sometimes as many as fifty, and stay there all winter long. The creeks may be covered with ice but there always seem to be patches of water here and there for them to swim in.

Because all of the leaves have fallen from deciduous shrubs and trees, the structure of the plants and the garden are quite visible. Winter is one of the best times to carefully look things over to see if you are happy with your landscape scheme. Gardeners call it winter gardening, and it doesn't necessarily mean planting or digging, but rather evaluating the backbone of your landscape—the trees and the shrubs, flower plantings, and general layout. Walk through the garden every few days and carefully and critically look it over for early spring projects. Take a notebook or diary with you and take notes. Do this consistently, and after a few years you will have a great deal of information about your garden stored away in the pages of your notebook. It will come in very handy throughout the year. Ask yourself,

"What should be moved? What should be removed? What should be planted?" Keep in mind that while plants are reasonably small and young, they can be moved easily and are more likely to survive the transplant shock. So if in doubt about the location or the aesthetics of a particular shrub or tree in your landscape, make a decision about it when first planting. It might be a good idea to wait for a season to replace it if that is what you have in mind. It will give you more time to think about exactly what you want in that spot.

Although winter is primarily a time to leave the garden on its own, there are a few chores which must be taken care of. It is always a good idea to mulch new plantings of perennials, shrubs, and ornamental trees with a covering of hay for the winter. This is because as the season wears on there are hot days and cold days. The ground around these plants freezes and thaws, which causes plants to heave from their planted position. There have been times when we have lost scores of plants to heaving. By applying a hay mulch *after* the ground is frozen, it will save you this disappointment and frustration.

In early to midwinter, the spring seed and plant catalogues begin to arrive. Again, walk around the garden and try to visualize what new plants you want to install. Or what seeds you want to plant under lights indoors for a head start. And remember this: Almost all gar-

The lacy pattern of silvery ice crystals in a pool of water resembles diamond-studded ferns.

The first snowfall of the season is always a knockout. Just look at the magic in this photo. Everything is draped in a blanket of snow.

deners overdo it when ordering plants during the winter, usually ordering far more than they either need or have time for. A rule of thumb is to make your list, and then cut it by one-third to one-half. And yes, you can live without that special magnolia for another year.

Even when the snow covers the garden with beauty, there are things that you must tend to. Snow, particularly wet snow, is heavy. In order to prevent unwanted breakage as the snow piles up on branches, you must knock the snow from them. Do this with a broom. Just walk through the garden with the broom and knock all the branches so that the snow falls to the ground and does not split or damage the trees and shrubs. If the snow is heavy and waterlogged, removing it is even more important if you do not want to lose some of your prized ornamentals. Dogwoods, franklinia, and birches are especially prone to breakage. It is great fun to get all bundled up and go out into the garden and beat the branches with a broom, and it also offers a little exercise during the indoor winter season.

Damage from ice storms is much harder to guard against. We are fortunate out on the East End for we rarely have severe ice storms. It is almost always either rain or snow. But having grown up in New Jersey, I know all about the damage that ice can do. Unfortunately, it is almost impossible to rid branches of heavy ice, unless you hose them down with warm water. You can brace some branches from below, but this is not a surefire way to prevent damage. I have yet to find or hear of one.

One of the most delightful pleasures of the winter garden is to go out and pick evergreen and holly branches to decorate the house during the holiday season. After a few years, as the plants grow, you will have more than enough to deck the hall. And what a nice pre-Christmas gift to give to friends. Sprays of holly and other berry-bearing plants and evergreens are always welcome gifts during the holidays. We take great pleasure in cutting greenery, lighting parts of the winter garden, and decorating the house during the holiday season. In fact, we even make our own wreaths now and look forward to it every year. Be sure to put that high on your list of spring planting. Beyond decorating, cutting branches during the holidays is a good way to prune any bush or tree.

Don't forget to feed the birds. But don't start to do so unless you are prepared to feed them all winter. If they get accustomed to coming to your feeders and find no food, they can die of starvation. It makes us feel good to do something special for the birds on holidays by placing some special treats at their feeding stations. Peanut butter smeared on tree bark or pinecones and raisins are favorites. They also like strings of popcorn. Be sure the suet feeders are filled and clean. On a Christmas morning, it is very lovely indeed to look out at the feeding area and see the feathered circus enjoying the special treats. Be sure to remember that birds, like all living things, need water. When everything is frozen solid, put out some fresh water for them. Inexpensive heating coils are available to keep the water from freezing.

Some of you may take this advice and some may not. For better or for worse, a month before Christmastime I begin to let everyone know that I don't want any Christmas gifts. I want New Year's gifts. And I don't want sweaters, gin, or upscale olive oil. I want trees and shrubs or gift certificates for them. And I want my friends and family to consult with me on what I want. I am bald-faced about it, pull no punches, and they are actually grateful because it saves them from trying to come up with something special year in and year out.

Since almost all of the annuals have finished blooming, been killed by frost, or gone into dormancy, there is little color in the winter garden. So you must plan ahead for a winter garden that offers some color and visual interest. Although dried grasses with their yellowish foliage and delicate, purple or white florescences, various sedums, and some pod-bearing perennials still offer some visual interest, almost all other flowering perennials and annuals are gone for the winter. Thus, shrubs and trees become the important visual focus of the winter garden. Both offer sculptural form and structure to the garden. As I said above, it is at this time that you can look over your landscape and decide where you feel you need more sculptural and structural interest because there are no leaves on the trees to distract from the purity of form. Many trees offer different kinds and colors of barks.

If you leave the spent flower heads on *Sedum* 'Autumn Joy,' as well as on Siberian iris and grasses, they take on a beauty all their own when poking up through the snow.

Feeding the birds is such a big part of winter in the country. Here a hungry chickadee stops at a hanging feeder for a snack of sunflower seeds; a male and female cardinal pause on the beautiful berry bush, with its brilliant purple blossoms; and a mourning dove waits. Mourning doves always seem to be waiting for something.

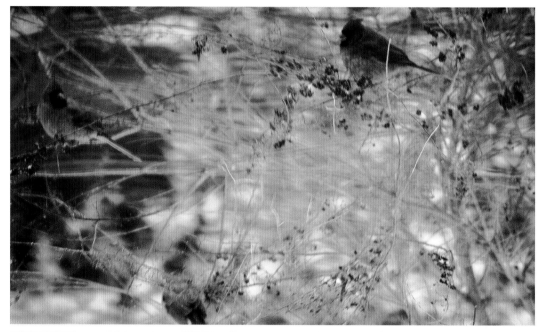

Birches offer white with an undercolor of deep rust, coral bark maple sports red branches, and some willows have yellow or red branches. Some barks are smooth, others are corky and rough. Without leaves the tree structure also becomes interesting. For example, the only interesting thing that Harry Lauder's walking stick offers is its twisted trunk and limb form. The conifers, or evergreens, bear cones, and their needle-like foliage comes in various shades of green, blue, white, yellow, ochre, and purple. Deciduous shrubs and trees have lost their autumn leaves but many offer brilliantly colored red, orange, yellow, white, bright purple, dark blue, and black berries to dress up the landscape, particularly after a snowfall. The berries gleam like beacons in the snow. And beyond their visual beauty, the birds love them and fill your garden with their colorful plumage. So this winter, look around your garden when you take a stroll and write down where you need visual interest. Then in spring, buy the plants you need and install them. Here are some that you will find interesting:

Acer palmatum 'Sango kaku' (coral bark maple), which grows from 10 to 15 feet, is a must-have in every garden. A tree of all seasons, in spring it sends out chartreuse green leaves lined with yellow, which then turn deep green and then brilliant yellow in the fall. In winter, the bark of the tree turns a brilliant red, stunning when snow-laden, and becomes the perfect place to hang a sunflower feeder to attract cardinals. At times we have had as many as twenty cardinals on the tree at once. That's almost as many as the pope has in the Vatican. It is a lovely sight to see during a gentle snowfall. We like this tree so much that we are planting two more this coming spring.

Callicarpa (beauty berry) is another must in any garden. It is a deciduous shrub grown for its unusual small clusters of bright purple berries that first appear in fall. After the leaves fall from the plant in early winter, the berries are brilliant and quite visible. It grows from 4 to 6 feet, but can be kept under control, if need be, by judicious pruning. A tough native plant, there are hybrids that have been developed that are more suitable for small gardens. These are the plants generally offered by nurseries. Beauty berry thrives in sun or partial shade in ordinary soil. Drought-resistant once established, it is a great addition to the winter garden.

Corylus avellana 'Contorta' (Harry Lauder's walking stick) is a tree that grows to 7 feet and its many branches are gnarled and contorted in fantastic ways. The twigs are also twisted. It is freakish looking but very interesting growing against a wall, and especially so if you prune out the twisted twigs. It is grown strictly for its bark and shape. Unless you are a

The bark of *Acer palmatum* 'Sango kaku' (coral bark maple) turns brilliant red in the winter, contrasting sharply with the surrounding snow. We hang sunflower feeders on it when it snows to attract brilliant red cardinals. ▦ A close-up of the purple berries that cover the *Callicarpa* (beauty bush) during the winter.

Like coral bark maple, the twigs of red osier dogwood, also called red-twig dogwood, turn scarlet in the winter.

show business buff, or are very chauvinistic about any Scottish background you might have, I am sure that you have never heard of Harry Lauder. He was a Scottish entertainer who performed during the early days of the nineteenth century. The tree was named after him.

Cornus sericea (red osier dogwood) is a deciduous native shrub, medium sized, multistemmed, and vase-shaped with rounded dark green leaves. It is grown primarily for its brilliant red bark, which colors in winter. This color is best when you cut back the shrub in late winter to encourage the production of young shoots for the following year's winter display. It does sport small white blossoms in late spring and white berries in summer, on medium green foliage, but they are quite inconsequential. Place one of these near a coral bark maple for a spectacular winter combination. *C. Sericea* 'Flaviramea' (golden-twig dogwood), the red osier's regal cousin, sports yellow stems.

Cotoneaster (cotoneaster) is a broad-leafed shrub. There is a wide range of cultivars, either upright or creeping, most with white or pink blossoms in spring and red berries in fall and winter, on lustrous, deep green foliage. Grows 2 to 20 feet, depending on variety. Most of them add brilliant color to the winter landscape, with either berries or foliage or both. They are drought-resistant once established. Here are some varieties that might interest you:

C. dammeri (bearberry cotoneaster) Low-growing (18 inches) and useful as a ground cover, although technically a shrub.

C. divaricatus (spreading cotoneaster) A carefree shrub that sports brilliant yellow and red long-lasting foliage in the winter. It grows to 6 feet.

C. horizontalis (rock spray cotoneaster) Another lower-growing variety (24 to 36 inches) that makes a beautiful winter display. A mature plant bears thousands of red berries.

C. salicifolius 'Autumn Fire' (willowleaf cotoneaster) offers interesting branching and winter displays of bright red or orange berries. It requires well-drained soil in the neutral range but is versatile, tolerating full sun or partial shade. This cultivar is small, only 2 to 3 feet high with silver-backed leaves. Glossy leaves are purplish in winter, and scarlet fruits persist.

Erica carnea (spring heath) are pretty little plants that grow to about 1 foot, gently spreading, with tiny, needle-like evergreen leaves. At the end of December and on into January, little spikes of white, pink, or red flowers bloom on the plant. Surely you have room for one of these to brighten the dreary days of mid- to late-winter. They like acid soil.

Euonymus fortunei (winter creeper) is a tough plant that stays evergreen all winter long. Leaves are 1 to 2½ inches long, often variegated, and very glossy. One plant will spread to 20 feet. They are drought-resistant and tolerate extremely cold temperatures. They will gently grow up large trees, covering the trunks with their attractive foliage. There is a yellow and green variety, another that has dark purple leaves in fall, and a gold-edged one that offers orange berries in the early winter.

Ilex (holly) There are many varieties that are wonderfully suited to the winter garden. All holly plants are either male or female, and as a rule both sexes must be present for the female to set those glorious brilliant red berries. But there are some that are self-fertile. Most hollies prefer rich, moist, slightly acid garden soil with good drainage. They grow in sun or partial shade, but produce the biggest berries in sunny areas. Here are some:

I. cornuta (Chinese holly) is a small evergreen shrub or tree. It tolerates heat and drought, growing ultimately to around 10 feet. Leaves are glossy and leathery, with spines at the four corners and at the tip. There are many varieties, all of which produce a great many red or yellow berries. The red are 'Berries Jubilee,' 'Burfordii,' and 'Dazzler.' The yellow are 'd'Or' and 'Rotunda,' which is a dwarf version of this cultivar. It is a compact grower to 3 to 4 feet wide, and is ideal for small gardens.

I. crenata (Japanese holly) is an evergreen holly that looks more like a boxwood than a holly. It grows to 8 feet and forms a fine dense hedge that can serve as a windbreak in the garden. Berries are black. It is not fussy about soil, light, or moisture. There are many varieties available, but 'Dwarf Pagoda' grows to only 1 foot in eight years, which makes it a good selection for a rock garden or small property.

I. x meserveae (Meserve hybrids) are a cross between English holly and a cold-tolerant species from northern

Some varieties of heath bloom in the dead of winter. Here a red variety looks stunning amid the pine needles and the snow.
■ This is a white-flowering heath, which also thrives and blooms in the winter.

If you have room for only one winter berry-bearing plant, choose a holly. It looks wonderful in the snow, and as the bush grows it provides plenty of greenery for decorating the house during the holidays. ■ We leave some of the garden ornaments outdoors during winter, particularly if they offer a whimsical touch when covered with snow. This bust of Michaelangelo's David looks like he's wearing a turban. ■ Our delightful marble cherub (*putti* in Italian) plays the cymbals, but not loud enough to scare away the birds. When we first got him, some of our grand friends wanted us to name him Wolfgang or Piero. We decided to name him Butch.

Japan. These are the hardiest of all hollies. Many varieties sport beautiful, glossy blue-green foliage. They grow from 6 to 7 feet tall. Some varieties are 'Blue Angel,' 'Blue Girl,' and 'Blue Princess.' If there is room for only one female holly plant in your garden, make it one of these. Male pollinators are 'Blue Boy' and 'Blue Prince.' Remember that you will need one of the male plants in order to have berries. After a few years this holly will supply you with all of the cuttings that you need for holiday decorations.

I. verticillata (common winterberry) is a native plant that comes from the swamps of eastern North America. In late fall and early winter, enormous crops of bright red berries that ripen to orange-red cover the plant. That is, unless the birds get them all, of course. Pollinators are required so be sure to plant a male pollinator close by. Consult your nursery or plant supplier for the details. Some varieties are 'Afterglow,' 'Fairfax,' 'Winter Red,' and 'Red Sprite.' *I. verticillata* 'Chrysocarapa' has yellow berries.

Kalmia latifolia (mountain laurel) is a superb winter shrub. Among broadleaf evergreens it is perhaps the only plant that can rival andromeda. Its growth habit is rounded and open, and the leathery leaves hold their deep green color throughout the winter. They do not curl back like rhododendron leaves when it gets cold.

Mahonia aquifolium (Oregon grape holly) is a tidy plant growing to 6 feet. Leaves are glossy green, turning purplish or bronze in the winter. 'Compacta' is the best selection for a small garden as it grows to only 2 feet tall and spreads freely. 'Orange Flame' grows to 5 feet and has wine red foliage in winter. In winter, both offer edible, blue-black berries which make good jelly.

Nandina domestica (heavenly bamboo) is of the barberry family, but unlike its cousins, it is not invasive. In late spring, creamy white spikes of flowers bloom on delicate, deep green, evergreen foliage. By fall, lush clusters of bright red blossoms cover the plant and the foliage turns from maroon to orange-red as the weather gets colder. The berries persist throughout the winter. It thrives in almost any kind of soil, in sun or shade. Drought resistant when established. Growing from 4 to 6 feet, it is a plant that is decorative in all seasons. It is particularly beautiful when planted as a companion to *Betula nigra* (river birch).

Pachysandra is about as "out" as any plant ever has or ever will be. However, it is an extremely useful and beautiful plant. The problem is that it was overdone in American suburbs after World War II. When I was a child, we had pachysandra filling in the foundation plantings and as ground cover all over the place. In fact, half of my hometown was paved with it. My mother would take pails of it to neighbors, to the point that they began to call her "Our Lady of the Pachysandra." At any rate, there comes a time in every gardener's life when nothing will help but pachysandra. When all else fails, pachysandra will thrive. It is almost totally maintenance free, always looks very elegant, fresh, and green, and also offers fragrant white flowers in the spring. Don't rule it out. It may turn out to be the best friend of the garden.

Pieris japonica (Japanese andromeda or lily-of-the-valley shrub) is one of the most versatile plants you can use in the winter garden. And it has visual interest all through the year. Whorls of leathery, lustrous oval leaves, with clusters of small, usually white, urn-shaped blossoms cover the plant. These flower buds, although not yet open, add winter interest to the plant. Much of the new foliage on an andromeda is reddish in color and many have red stems in the winter, giving it a reddish hue. This contrasts stunningly with a blanket of snow. In late winter or very early spring, pendulous clusters of creamy white flowers, like those of lily of the valley, cover the plant.

Pyracantha coccinea (scarlet firethorn) is a broad-leafed evergreen shrub. In summer, clusters of white flowers bloom over evergreen or semievergreen foliage. It is a dazzling addition to the winter garden because of its stunning red or orange berries, which it is primarily used for. It can be espaliered against a fence. It grows from 6 to 18 feet and thrives in

Nandina is a form of noninvasive bamboo and is covered with these stunning red-orange berries throughout the winter and into the spring.

Clockwise from top left: A gardener friend leaves her blue mirror reflecting ball out in the snow. It certainly is a focal point and adds interest to an otherwise ordinary winter landscape. ■ *Pyracantha* (firethorn) is a fabulous plant for a winter garden. It is covered with brilliant orange berries and can be espaliered against a wall or a fence. ■ We have high pruned this privet hedge so that the trunks form interesting patterns against the fence behind it. ■ This view of our garden, taken from the pond area, shows our little barn adorned with a Christmas wreath. In the summer, the barn serves as a disco when we have wild parties.

well-drained soil in full sun. Control growth by judicious annual pruning. A spectacular addition to the fall garden.

Rosa (rose) Both *R. hugonis* (Father Hugo rose), with its single, canary yellow flowers that bloom in early summer, and our native *R. virginiana* (Virginia rose) with its 2- to 3-inch pink blossoms in early summer, put on quite a display in winter with their rose hips. And it's fun to pick them in the snow and then come inside and make some rose hip jelly out of them. That is, if you like rose hip jelly.

Skimmia is a handsome plant that only recently took its place in our winter garden. It grows in a low mound and has very nice little, broadleaf evergreen foliage. In spring it offers clusters of white blossoms that are fragrant, and in early winter, dull red, holly-like fruits that last through the season. Plant both male and female varieties as they must cross-pollinate. Skimmia thrives in shade, making it very useful in shady areas.

Vaccinium corymbosum (highbush blueberry) One of the best plants for the winter landscape, because like the coral bark maple, the twigs of this tree turn a beautiful red in the cold. Acid soil is preferred, and the cultivar provides interest throughout the year. In spring, white to pink flowers bloom, followed by delicious blueberries in summer and then scarlet foliage in the fall. Birds love the blueberries, so net the tree if you want to have them yourself.

Taxus (yew) We have to include this because we have what we have been told is the oldest living yew on Long Island. It stands about 30 feet high. In the fall, brilliant red berries cover the tree. The birds love them, but they are poisonous to human beings so don't be tempted to eat them. As I often say of our magnificent tree, this is what happens when you don't prune a yew bush.

There are only a handful of plants that bloom in the depths of winter. *Helleborus niger* (Christmas rose) and *Helleborus orientalis* (Lenten rose) are two. They are evergreen and grow to about 18 inches tall, spread tidily, and sport 2-inch single flowers with five petals. The Christmas version begins to bloom about a week before Christmas, with the Lenten version blooming in mid-February. These often poke their blossoms up through the snow, but do not be alarmed because they are very tough and are not affected by cold temperatures. They are a godsend to the winter garden; in fact, hybridizers have created scores of new varieties that have become available in the past few years. They range in color from white to pink, yellow, purple, mahogany, green, and combinations thereof. And they require next to no attention. Just plant them in a shady spot in soil that you have fortified with a large amount of humus or rotted compost. Water them during summer drought.

Other plants that start blooming in January or February are the drabas, *Primula vulgaris* (primrose), arabis, creeping myrtle, and *Pulmonaria* (lungwort). Drabas are alpine plants with small clusters of brilliant yellow flowers on top of gray-green foliage. Primroses offer yellow, rust, red, and blue-colored clusters of blossoms on 8-inch-high stems over rosettes of medium green foliage. Arabis grows in mat form, with gray-green leaves and is usually covered with clusters of white blossoms from late February into April. Creeping myrtle spreads vigorously, with 1-inch-long, glossy, deep green leaves, and small periwinkle blue blossoms as soon as there is a warm day in January. *Pulmonaria* offers speckled foliage and blossoms in bright blue, pink, or white, and also serves as a handsome ground cover. It is an excellent late-winter and early-spring plant because the blooming persists well into April and the foliage is attractive all year round. There are a few shrubs that bloom in mid-winter. *Hamamelis* (witch hazel) is one. It is a small deciduous tree or tall shrub that bears

129

The earliest blooming of all shrubs, *Hamamelis* (witch hazel) sports these ribbon-like, buttery yellow blossoms in the middle of winter. As an added bonus, the fall foliage is brilliant red or orange.

yellow, ribbon-like flower petals, often fragrant in late winter. It is usually the first of all shrubs to bloom. There are many bulbs that do appear in late winter.

After the holidays, in order to brighten up the house, try cutting some shrub branches for forcing. Undoubtedly you know that you can cut forsythia and pussy willow and force them, but there are so many other shrubs that you can force as well. Here is a list of them, according to the months when they can be picked. All should be placed in a pail of water in a dark place until they sprout and bud and then brought out into the light to enjoy.

January: Gable hybrid azaleas, azaleas, Exbury azaleas, Korean rhododendrons, Kurume azaleas, forsythia, witch hazel, flowering peach, flowering cherry, flowering plum

February: Japanese scarlet quince, forsythia, saucer magnolia, flowering cherry, pussy willow, Korean rhododendron

March: flowering dogwood, quince, deutzia, forsythia, crabapple, spiraea, lilac, and fruit trees such as apple, peach, plum, and pear. Pink apricot blossoms have one of the loveliest scents of all flowers. It is worthwhile to plant a dwarf apricot just for the spring blossoms.

As the last snowfalls of March melt into the past and the annual miracle of spring is only a few weeks away, we come to the end of a year in the life of a garden. There is always that last gasp of winter that sends the snow swirling and the winds whirling while the garden is snug, warm, and asleep under the soft snow. Although the snow-laden, slope-shouldered shrubs appear to affect the "debutante slouch" of another era, it is our magnificent 150-year-old yew tree that once again steals the show as it becomes a glorious and enormous sculpture that almost boisterously invites you to participate in its new beauty by walking around and under it, and even climbing it. It gracefully bows under the weight of a blanket of white. Like a prima ballerina wrapped in ermine, winter takes its curtain calls after its farewell performance.

Helleborus niger (Christmas rose) starts blooming around Christmastime and continues on through the spring. Visitors are always surprised to see their lovely blooms in the dead of winter. ▉ In our area, the last rose of summer often blooms in December. Here is a cluster of pink climbing roses successfully weathering an early snowfall. ▉ Our 150-year-old yew tree, still the masterpiece of the garden, takes its final bow after a late-winter storm.